Utah Women and the Law

Utah Women and the Law

The Utah Governor's Commission
on the
Status of Women

Bonneville Books
University of Utah Press
Salt Lake City
1986

Printed in the United States of America

Library of Congress Cataloging-in-Publication Data

Utah women and the law.

(Bonneville books)
Includes index.
1. Women—Legal status, law, etc.—Utah. 1. Utah.
Governor's Commission on the Status of Women.
KFU91.W6A87 1987 342.792'0878 87-5075
ISBN 0-87480-301-2 (pbk.) 347.9202878

STATE OF UTAH
OFFICE OF THE GOVERNOR
SALT LAKE CITY
84114

NORMAN H. BANGERTER
GOVERNOR

Greetings!

This handbook on legal issues concerning women is the result of six years of volunteer effort under two different administrations. It is a good example of filling a need through hard work and perseverance. I would like to commend all of the past and current members of the Governor's Commission on the Status of Women, and other volunteers who gave so generously of their time and talents to bring this dream to fruition.

While the handbook is by no means a complete legal resource, or a substitute for professional legal advice, it will hopefully serve as a valuable guide on issues relating to women's legal rights and responsibilities in the state of Utah.

I sincerely hope that the women of Utah who read "Utah Women and the Law: A Resource Handbook" will find it informative and helpful as they address various concerns that affect them and their families.

Many thanks to all who participated in this worthwhile effort.

Sincerely,

Norman H. Bangerter
Governor

Contents

Major funding for
Utah Women and the Law: A Resource Handbook
was provided by

RAY, QUINNEY, AND NEBEKER FOUNDATION
THE UTAH BAR FOUNDATION
and
GRETHE AND CHASE PETERSON

Additional funding was provided by the Order of Women Legislators, the Intermountain Commercial Record, Gateway League of Utah, Utah Business and Professional Women, and Alice Durrant, Utah Women, Inc.

Preface

Utah Women and the Law: A Resource Handbook is a project of the Utah Governor's Commission on the Status of Women. Its purpose is to provide an overview of the legal statutes that deal with the most common problems faced by women and to suggest agencies to contact and questions to ask. This handbook is intended to be a practical guide on basic legal matters but by no means should be considered a substitute for competent legal counsel.

Plans for the handbook were first outlined in 1979. Most of the material was written from 1984 to 1986. The handbook is a compilation of writings, by experts in the areas addressed, who generously contributed their legal expertise and hard work. Members of the Governor's Commission on the Status of Women and a number of additional legal experts also contributed to the preparation of this document. Their services were invaluable in its development, publication, funding, and distribution.

Utah Woman and the Law: A Resource Handbook is dedicated to the women of Utah. The inspiration for its publication came from an awareness of the courage and determination demonstrated by Utah women to live worthwhile lives and to actively seek better conditions and circumstances for themselves and others.

Acknowledgments

A project such as this reflects the professional expertise and personal compassion of literally dozens of people who have felt the need of Utah's women for a better understanding of how they relate to the legal system. We gratefully recognize the hundreds of hours volunteered to complete *Utah Women and the Law: A Resource Handbook*.

The main chapter authors identified the relevant statutes and cases, wrote them in lay terms, and spelled out their implications.

Chapter 1, "Finding a Lawyer"—*Sue Ann Walker*, attorney at law, Salt Lake County Attorney's Office, Salt Lake City, Utah; and *Jaynne Allison*, attorney at law, formerly of Vancott, Bagley, Cornwall & McCarthy, Salt Lake City, Utah.

Chapter 2, "Utah Divorce Law"—*Brian M. Bernard*, attorney at law, Utah Legal Clinic, Salt Lake City, Utah. *Kathryn Collard*, attorney at law, Salt Lake City, Utah contributed.

Chapter 3, "Property Rights"—*Brenda L. Flanders*, attorney at law, Salt Lake City, Utah.

Chapter 4, "Money Problems and Bankruptcy"—*Barbara W. Richman*, attorney at law, Richman and Richman, Salt Lake City, Utah.

Chapter 5, "Taxes"—*A. Gayle Brice*, Group Manager, Examination Section, Internal Revenue Service, Salt Lake City, Utah.

Chapter 6, "Social Welfare Laws"—*Anne Milne*, Director, Utah Legal Services, Inc., Salt Lake City, Utah.

Chapter 7, "Employment"—*Karen Suzuki-Hashimoto*, formerly of the Utah State Personnel Management Office, now Personnel Director, FHP, Salt Lake City, Utah. *Chizuko Ishimatsu*, former member of the Utah Governor's Commission on the Status of Women, and *Kathryn Collard*, attorney at law, Salt Lake City, contributed initial research on this chapter.

Chapter 8, "Education"—*Jan L. Tyler*, Ph.D., Director of Human Resource Management and Organization Development, Utah State Department of Social Services, Salt Lake City, Utah; *Kaye M. Coleman*, Ph.D., Associate Director of the Office of Equal Opportunity, University of Utah, Salt Lake City, Utah; and *Barbara B. Hales*, Specialist, Vocational Equity, Utah State Office of Education, Salt Lake City, Utah.

Chapter 9, "Mental and Physical Health"—*Jane Reister Conard*, Assistant Counsel, Intermountain Health Care, Inc., Salt Lake City, Utah, wrote the section on mental health while *Linda Stengel Lepreau*, attorney at law, Salt Lake City; Utah, and *Kathryn Collard*, attorney at law, Salt Lake City, Utah, wrote various sections on physical health.

Chapter 10, "Women and Criminal Justice"—*Karen Knight-Eagan*, Deputy County Attorney, Salt Lake County Attorney's Office, Salt Lake City, Utah. *Kathryn Collard,* attorney at law, Salt Lake City, Utah, contributed research.

Chapter 11, "Children: Adoption, Support, Protection, Rights of Minors, and Education for the Handicapped"—*Mimi S. Buescher*, attorney at law, former Assistant City Prosecutor, Office of the Salt Lake City Prosecutor. *Michael Dazey*, former attorney with the Utah Legal Center for the Handicapped, Salt Lake City, Utah, furnished research on education laws related to the handicapped.

Chapter 12, "Jury Duty"—*Sue Ann Walker*, attorney at law, Salt Lake County Attorney's Office, Salt Lake City, Utah.

Chapter 13, "Women and the Military"—*Paul M. Warner*, Associate Deputy Attorney General, State of Utah, and major with the Judge Advocate General Corps, Utah Army National Guard.

Chapter 14, "Utah's Equal Rights Statute"—*Sue Ann Walker*, attorney at law, Salt Lake County Attorney's Office, Salt Lake City, Utah.

We thank those who assisted in research for the chapters and analysis of particular sections, including John Medina, Director of the Anti-Discrimination Division for the State of Utah; Stephen Bonney, Executive Director of Utah Health Systems Agency; the staff attorneys of Utah Legal Services; Sandra Wiens-Bagley, M.S.W., Ph.D.; Vera Callister Badham, attorney at law; and Rae Harder, Kim Luhn, Tammy Prince, Chris Brislin, Sally McMinimee, Eileen Otti, Olga Bruno, Joy Douglas, Vicki Johnson, and Diane Abegglen, the Association of Women Law Students at the College of Law, University of Utah, who checked citations.

Our technical staff merit our warm appreciation: Lavina Fielding Anderson of Editing, Inc., for the editing; and Patricia Durrant of Accuracy Plus for typing the manuscript.

While all members of the Utah Governor's Commission on the Status of Women have contributed to the creation of this handbook, the following commissioners deserve particular thanks for their involvement in this project: Christine Fitzgerald Soltis, attorney at law, who chaired the Law Handbook Committee, Sherrill G. Box, Alice Durrant, Ione Simpson, Margaret May, Grethe B. Peterson, and Pamela M. Winder. Also deserving recognition for work on this project are Ruth Hardy Funk, the chairperson of the commission during many of the years when the handbook took shape, and her successor Valerie Kelly, who worked with great dedication to move the handbook toward publication during her tenure, ended by her death in an automobile accident in February 1986.

Sincere thanks are due former Governor Scott M. Matheson and Governor Norman Bangerter who encouraged and supported the creation of this handbook.

Kathleen Criddle Mason, Chair
Utah Governor's Commission
on the Status of Women,
December, 1986

Commissioners During Development of Handbook

Former Commissioners

Jaynne Allison
Christine Burdick
Sherrill Box
Marta D. Clark
Alice Durrant
Julia A. Fry
Ruth Hardy Funk
Chizuko Ishimatsu
Nancy Stowe Kader
Valeria Kelly
Elma Klitgaard
Jan Cromar Lewis
Mary L. Olsen
Catherine Peck
Marybeth Raynes
Ione J. Simpson
Genalee May Shuman
Christine F. Soltis
Joo Sim Tan
Meg Terrell
Jan Tyler

Present Commissioners

Barbara B. Hales
Doris G. Hall
Shirley R. Johnsen
Jinnah Kelson
Lorraine N. MacKay
Kathleen C. Mason
Noemi P. Mattis
Bonnie G. Miller
Grethe B. Peterson
Marianne Stoddard
Olene S. Walker
Ruth T. Walker
Beverly J. White
Margaret D. Wilson
Pamela M. Winder
Betty Tatham and Carol Clark (Governor's representatives to the commission)

1 Finding A Lawyer

WHAT SHOULD I DO IF I NEED A LAWYER AND DON'T KNOW ANY?

If you need to enforce or defend your legal rights—rights that are described in the rest of this book—visit or call the Utah State Bar's Lawyer Referral Office at 425 East 100 South, Salt Lake City, UT 84111. The phone number is 531-9075.

When you tell the people in this office what your particular problem is, they will give you the names, phone numbers, and addresses of attorneys who work in those specific legal areas. When you call an attorney for an appointment, say you were referred by the Utah State Bar. The attorney is obligated to meet with you at a cost of $15 for the first half-hour consultation. Be sure you discuss fees if it looks as if you will work together, for the $15 limit applies only to the first visit.

WHAT SHOULD I KNOW ABOUT ATTORNEYS' FEES?

You should not hesitate to call a lawyer and inquire about the fee for consultation. You will not be charged for this initial phone conversation. Lawyers have a variety of fee arrangements available depending on the type of case and the client's financial circumstances. Whichever arrangement you and your lawyer agree upon, make sure you have a clear understanding of what the fee will be and get a fee agreement in writing.

Some of the more common types of fee arrangements are the flat fee, the hourly rate, and the contingent fee.

The flat fee is a specific amount of money for which a lawyer agrees to perform specific legal services. For example, a lawyer may charge a flat fee of $300 for a simple, uncontested divorce, a flat fee of $600 to incorporate your small business, or a flat fee of $50 to draft a simple will. A flat fee arrangement usually implies that the lawyer will render the "customary and necessary" legal services that another lawyer in the same area would render in the same kind of case. It is very important that you and your lawyer have a clear agreement in writing as to what a flat fee does and does not cover.

Sometimes there is no way of knowing at the outset what a particular legal matter will involve. In cases where a lawyer cannot accurately gauge or estimate a total fee, an hourly rate is often the best arrangement. An hourly fee might also be desirable when a client wishes to have a lawyer do some preliminary research and give a legal opinion regarding a matter (for example, whether to bring suit). Hourly fees charged by lawyers vary widely, so be sure to have a clear understanding of the fixed rate per hour before agreeing to pay a lawyer an hourly fee.

Contingent fee arrangements allow clients to pursue lawsuits that might otherwise be impossible. They are often used in negligence, personal injury and collection cases, to name a few. (They are illegal in divorce or criminal cases.) A lawyer who takes a case on a contingency basis usually does so because the client has limited financial resources and the lawyer feels that there is a good chance that he or she can win the case.

In a contingent fee arrangement, a lawyer takes a fee only if money is recovered. If so, the lawyer's fee will be an agreed-upon percentage of the amount recovered. If your case produces no money, the lawyer is not paid for time and services. The client, however, must bear all "costs" and "expenses" related to the case.

Lawyers' percentages in contingent fee arrangements are high, ranging from about one-third to as much as half. If you enter such an arrangement, make sure the agreement is spelled out in writing. Be sure you understand what the percentage is, on what amount it will be calculated, and what "costs" and "expenses" you will be responsible for.

WHAT IF I CAN'T AFFORD A LAWYER?

Many services are still available. The American Civil Liberties Union specializes in problems based upon violations of civil liberties (like your right to free speech) or discrimination (if you've been fired so they can hire a man, for instance). If your case falls within their range of interests and would clarify the law in what they consider to be a needed area, they may assign an attorney to represent you without charge, no matter what your economic status or family income may be. The ACLU is located in the Judge Building, 8 East

Broadway, Suite 615, Salt Lake City, UT 84111. The phone number is 521-9289.

Another group offering legal services for a special kind of case is the Legal Center for the Handicapped at 254 West 400 South, Suite 300, Salt Lake City, UT 84111. The phone number is 363-1347. This office provides legal services to people who are developmentally disabled, meaning that they have a chronic mental or physical disability which was present before age twenty-one and is likely to continue indefinitely. Their fees are based on family income and range from no charge to around $15 for each consultation.

There are two groups that will help you with legal services of a more general nature. The Legal Aid Society at 231 East 400 South in Salt Lake City, UT 84111 (328-8849) will provide legal assistance based on family income. Call the Legal Aid Society for information regarding income guidelines, as each case is evaluated individually. This office serves only residents of Salt Lake County and specializes in problems involving domestic and family law—like child custody, divorce and similar matters.

The Legal Aid Society works closely with another agency, Utah Legal Services, Inc., at 637 East 400 South, Salt Lake City, UT 84102 (328-8891). The Legal Aid Society will refer to Utah Legal Services most of its cases involving income maintenance (i.e., welfare payments, Medicaid, aid to dependent children, Supplemental Security Income, etc.), landlord-tenant disputes and immigration problems. Utah Legal Services will, in turn, refer most of its family law cases back to the Legal Aid Society. However, Legal Aid operates only in Salt Lake County while Utah Legal Services, Inc. has offices in Salt Lake, Provo, Ogden, and Cedar City. Utah Legal Services charges no fee, but provides services only to the poor. The National Legal Services Corporation sets income guidelines based on the family's gross monthly income and the number of people supported by that income.

WHAT CAN A LAWYER DO FOR ME?

Since you are not a lawyer, you may not be aware of how much a lawyer can do to help you in some circumstances. A lawyer can help keep you out of legal trouble, assure that your legal transactions are handled properly, or assist you if you should get into legal difficulty. Some of life's transactions should never be undertaken without a lawyer. Among these are getting a divorce, adopting a child, buying or selling property, filing for bankruptcy, making or changing a will, starting a business, facing a lawsuit against you, or suing someone else. You should avoid assuming that you don't need a lawyer. It is almost never too late to find out what a lawyer can do for you.

WHAT IF I'M ARRESTED?

You still get a lawyer if you need one and want one whether you can afford to hire one or not. If you're arrested, you are taken to the police station and "booked," meaning that your name and alleged crime are written in a ledger. You are photographed, fingerprinted and placed in a cell. What do you do now?

You have a right to make at least two telephone calls to your family, friends, or lawyer. When you were arrested, you should have been informed of your constitutional rights to remain silent and to speak with a lawyer before answering any questions relating to the case.

Once you have been arrested, you can be held in jail only for a short time while legal formalities are carried out. You must then be taken without unnecessary delay before a judge for "arraignment" (the first court appearance). At the time of the arraignment, the judge will read the charges against you, set the conditions for releasing you from jail until your trial (either bail or on your own recognizance) and ask you whether you have a lawyer. Anyone arrested or otherwise accused of a serious crime (i.e., any jailable offense) is entitled to a lawyer. If you cannot afford to hire one, the state or federal government has funds to provide one for you at no cost if you meet certain guidelines relative to your income and other financial resources. If the judge feels that you need a lawyer, he or she will order that one be assigned to you and determine whether you should pay any fees. Your attorney will be assigned by Legal Defenders, 333 South 200 East, Salt Lake City, UT 84111, 532-5444.

WHAT IF I'M ARRAIGNED IN A COURT THAT'S NOT IN SALT LAKE CITY?

Arraignment takes place in the county where you were arrested. Once you are released on bail or on your own recognizance, you may return to your home until time for your trial (or other court appearances). According to Utah law, criminal trials are held in the county where the crime is said to have occurred.

2 Utah Divorce Law

HOW DO I START DIVORCE PROCEEDINGS?

Since marriage is a legal contract, sanctioned by the state, it must be legally dissolved. When wife or husband feels that the terms of the marriage contract have been broken, either one can file for divorce in the state district court of the county in which either has resided for the last three months.[1] (Every state has a residency requirement. Utah's is in the middle between Nevada—six weeks—and California—six months.)

However, there must be reasons or "grounds" for the divorce that meet the requirements of Utah divorce laws, which have been set by statutes enacted by the legislature. The current grounds have been in effect for many years and are similar to those enacted in most states. Some states (California, for instance) within the last decade or so have enacted "no-fault" statutory grounds for divorce ("irreconcilable differences," for example). Utah has not.

WHAT HAPPENS IN DIVORCE PROCEEDINGS?

We'll describe the procedure as if you were filing for a divorce, making you the plaintiff and your husband the defendant. If your husband were to file, then you'd be the defendant and he'd be the plaintiff. For the legal divorce process to begin, you must file a complaint with the clerk of the court.

The terms of the complaint are drafted by your attorney based on your answers to questions like these: How much support do you need? What share of the property do you want or would be fair? What is your husband's income? Is alimony appropriate? etc.

The current (1986) filing fee is $77. The complaint sets forth the factual situation and reasons for the divorce, the agreements the couple has already made, if any (about custody and property, for instance), and what other items must be resolved between the parties.

Next, your husband must be given "notice" (a summons) of the divorce action. A sheriff or constable may serve (personally hand-deliver to) the notice to your husband. This is called formal service. Or your lawyer may mail a copy to your husband, telling him of the action and enclosing a copy of the complaint. This is called informal service.

In formal service, your husband has twenty days to file an answer or propose a compromise or modification. With informal service, he must respond within a reasonable time or be formally served. The answer sets out what the defendant agrees to and disagrees with. Often an answer and counterclaim are filed simultaneously. A counterclaim is a counter-suit. In it your husband says, "Wait. You treated *me* cruelly, and I deserve a divorce from *you*." In the answer and/or counterclaim, he sets forth how he thinks the issues should be resolved about custody of children, support, property division, etc.

In response to a counterclaim, your attorney will file a reply, which is the equivalent of your husband's answer: you agree to such-and-such items in the counterclaim and disagree with others.

Please don't try to deal with a divorce without at least consulting a lawyer. Even if you think you agree to all of the terms in the complaint, you can benefit from the experience of someone who knows the process. If your husband has had his complaint served formally, it is essential to have an attorney. Formal service almost always means that your husband is planning to be aggressive and noncooperative.

If your husband wants to contest (disagree with) the divorce or its terms and files an answer to which compromise or negotiation is not acceptable, the matter goes to trial. At a trial, all of the facts will be presented to the judge who will make the final decision as to whether a divorce should be granted, who should get custody, whether alimony should be awarded, if so, what amount, what amount of child support should be ordered, who gets what property, etc.

Before the matter goes to trial, in a contested divorce, both lawyers will engage in "discovery." Discovery is a method of "discovering" facts and information about the litigation and other side's position. For instance, your husband might want to find out about your retirement plan and how much it is worth; he'd subpoena the retirement records from the employer. You might want to find out more about the partnership your husband is involved in; you would subpoena the records from that business for your attorney to review. If there is a fight over custody, discovery usually involves a "custody evaluation"—a home study and review by a social worker, psychologist, etc., and an expert recommendation to the court about who can best care for the children, etc.

Once both parties have had a chance to do "discovery," a process that usually takes several months, the matter is presented to the judge at a trial. After hearing all of the facts, the judge then makes a decision about every item in dispute. That final decision is embodied in a written legal document known as the decree. The decree is the final order that legally terminates the marriage and resolves the various disputes.

Many times the parties can agree and resolve certain disputes before the trial—for example, Janet will have custody of the five children—but cannot agree on related issues. How much child support should Jay pay? Should Janet have possession of the house until the youngest child reaches the age of eighteen? They will tell the judge at the beginning of the trial exactly what is in dispute and the court will direct its attention only to those items.

Over 95 percent of the divorces in Utah do *not* go to trial. Most divorces are either uncontested or negotiated and settled before trial, but you still need a lawyer. Although both of you may want a divorce, it is still a legal matter.

In a simple, uncontested divorce, you (if you're the plaintiff) file the divorce action and deliver a copy of the complaint to your husband. He reviews the complaint and finds that he can agree to all of the terms. He then signs a short legal document variously called an acceptance, waiver, or consent before a notary public. That acceptance says that the defendant accepts and agrees to the terms as set forth in the complaint. The signed and notarized acceptance is filed with the court. The court then allows you to present grounds, etc., and to be granted the divorce.

In a more complicated no-trial divorce, your husband does not agree to all of the terms in the complaint. Negotiations begin, with or without filing an answer. Negotiations would be along the lines of:

"If you want $200 a month for each of our six kids, I cannot pay all of the bills. I'll pay all the bills if you'll lower the support to $150 per month."

"I'll lower the support to $150 per month, but instead of you getting one-half of the equity when I sell the house, you'll only get one-third."

"My retirement is not worth anything because I cannot get to it or use it until I'm 65+, so I don't think it is fair that you should get all of the equity in the house and I should get only my retirement plan. You're able to use the home equity right now." Etc.

These negotiations may go on for months and may result in the parties being able to reach a written agreement or "settlement stipulation" resolving all disputed items. If that is the case, the plaintiff will go to court, present the settlement along with grounds, etc., and the court will grant the divorce in the same manner as an uncontested divorce.

This negotiation process may also result in resolving many issues before trial but leave a few you can't agree on for the judge to consider at a trial. Sometimes the negotiations result in a settlement right at the courthouse door, just before trial.

Most divorce attorneys will work hard to negotiate and settle a case before trial. The judge's decision usually is "fair" (a forced compromise) from the view of a disinterested third party, but a negotiated settlement is usually better because you can be involved in developing your own compromise.

After a divorce action (the complaint) has been filed, it is considered pending until there can be a hearing. Since you must wait three months (a period set by law) before even a "default" hearing (appearing before the judge to orally present grounds), it is often necessary to seek a temporary order regarding custody, child support, etc.

WHAT ARE THE GROUNDS FOR DIVORCE IN UTAH?

Currently, Utah law says that one spouse must be at fault for a divorce to be granted. This means that one spouse must blame or find fault with the other to establish legal grounds or reasons for a divorce. Some states have "no-fault" divorce laws which allow divorce when there are "irreconcilable differences" or when a couple can no longer "pursue the legitimate purposes of the marriage." No-fault laws mean couples do not have to assign blame but can simply tell the court that the marriage is no longer working.

When "irreconcilable differences" are grounds for a divorce, the plaintiff may be specifically forbidden by law from telling the judge anything more regarding grounds than just saying, "We have determined that there are irreconcilable differences between us and we want our marriage legally dissolved." Thus "irreconcilable differences" means whatever the parties want it to mean.

All of the statutory grounds for divorce in Utah would probably fall in the category of "irreconcilable differences." The nice thing about "irreconcilable differences" as grounds is that you don't have to reveal to a judge or the court why you want your marriage dissolved; those reasons are really no one else's business. The state didn't ask you why you wanted to get married. The state should not ask you why you want to terminate your marriage.

Under the traditional application of the fault concept in securing divorces, the offending party might have been "punished" by losing access to the children, being awarded a smaller portion of the marital property, etc. Such judgments may still be made, of course, but not solely on the basis of the grounds for the divorce.

Current Utah law says legal reasons or grounds for a divorce[2] are:

1. Impotency at the time of marriage.
2. Adultery committed after the marriage.
3. Desertion of the spouse for more than one year.
4. Failure to provide the "common necessities of life." This means, basically, refusal to support you. This ground would be established if your husband moves out and you have to seek public assistance. Because of the fault concept used in Utah, this ground would probably require that your husband have the ability to support and then fail to do so. If he were physically disabled, for instance, and could not support the family, this ground probably would not apply.
5. Habitual drunkenness. This conduct also overlaps with the category of "mental cruelty"; thus, there is no need to get specific. If you can say "My husband has used alcohol to excess" or "My husband's consumption of alcohol creates problems between us," that constitutes mental cruelty.
6. Conviction, or being found guilty of a felony, a serious crime for which a person can be sentenced to prison for more than one year. Examples are murder, rape, burglary, robbery, possession or sale of large quantities of illicit drugs, etc.
7. Mental or physical cruelty, that is, cruel treatment that causes bodily injury or great mental distress.
8. Being legally separated by a court decree for three years in a row. A legal separation or separate maintenance decree is described later.

9. Permanent and incurable insanity, which must be established by actual court-ordered commitment to a hospital, or by competent medical testimony.

If you want a divorce in Utah, you will be required to discuss confidential details of your marriage and personal life with the court.

Nearly all of the people who ask for a divorce in Utah give "mental cruelty" as the reason. When a couple is incompatible or "the legitimate ends of the marriage are no longer being served," specific acts of mental cruelty are present and are grounds for divorce.

WHAT IS THE DIFFERENCE BETWEEN A LEGAL SEPARATION AND A DIVORCE IN UTAH?

Parties are "legally separated" only when a court has entered a decree of separate maintenance, a court order which divides property, provides support, etc. Based upon a determination by the parties that they cannot live together, the court enters an order to resolve questions of property, support, etc., without terminating the marriage. The order tells the parties to live separately, specifies who gets what property, who pays what support, which party is responsible for which bills, which children will live with which parent, etc.[3]

To obtain a decree of separate maintenance in Utah, a couple must go through a proceeding very much like a divorce. A decree of separate maintenance divides property, awards custody of children, and provides for child support and alimony—but only for a temporary period of time. A decree of separate maintenance may stay in effect until the death of either party or until one or the other seeks a divorce. There is no limit to the duration.

The decree of separate maintenance does not legally end the marriage. Alimony is more common under a decree of separate maintenance than under a divorce decree because the parties are still legally married, and the law requires a husband to support his wife.

The paper work, attorney's fees, and court costs for a legal separation are about the same as for a divorce. If, after a legal separation is decreed the couple decide they want a divorce, attorney and court fees must be paid again for the divorce. However, living under a decree of separate maintenance for three years as grounds for divorce is the closest grounds in Utah to a "no-fault" divorce.

HOW DO I GET A LEGAL SEPARATION IN UTAH?

You hire an attorney to file a complaint for a legal separation, just as you would for a divorce. In Utah, the statutory grounds for separate maintenance are the same for both men and women.

Current grounds:

1. When a spouse has deserted you without good and sufficient cause, or
2. If he could support you but either neglected or refused to "properly provide for and suitably maintain" you, or
3. When he lives away from you through no fault of yours, or
4. Is sentenced to the state prison for a year or more.

There is no three-month residency requirement to seek a decree of separate maintenance but you must be a resident (no specific duration).[4]

WHAT ARE THE LEGAL REASONS FOR AN ANNULMENT IN UTAH?

An annulment is a court decision that a marriage was not valid at the time it took place. It means the marriage never existed legally, unlike a divorce which dissolves a previously legal and valid marriage.[5]

The two most common grounds for annulment are "lack of capacity" and fraud. "Lack of capacity" means that for some reason a person was legally incapable of marrying—that he or she was under legal age (see next question) or still married to another person, mentally defective, or so drunk that he or she didn't know what he or she was doing.

To prove that one of these conditions existed, a court will sometimes accept your husband's admission. For instance, when he is served with the complaint for an annulment, he does not respond and does not deny the grounds. Proof that a previous divorce was not final could be made by showing the court a copy of the decree. Proof that he was under age and did not have parental permission could be made by a copy of a birth certificate and a copy of the marriage license without a parent's signature.

Proof that a person was incapacitated and not acting in awareness could be her own testimony, for instance, "We had been drinking for three days and taking pills. I remember going to Elko but can't remember anything after that. When we got back to Salt Lake, and I sobered up, Lawrence told me we were married and showed me a marriage license."

Fraud as grounds for annulment must be a "substantial and material untruth" which actually affects someone's decision to marry. If a person conceals the fact of several previous marriages or if a woman tells her prospective husband she is pregnant with his child when she is not, fraud would be involved.

Other grounds for annulment in Utah are that a spouse has a communicable venereal disease or the marriage ceremony was not performed by an authorized person.[6]

Another reason for annulment is kinship. When parties are cousins or "closer," the marriage is incestuous and void. Uncle and niece are "closer," so are "blood"-related brothers and sisters, and half-brothers and half-sisters.[7]

WHAT IS THE LEGAL AGE FOR MARRIAGE IN UTAH?

In Utah, a man or woman under the age of fourteen cannot legally marry. If either a man or woman is under the age of sixteen, a marriage between them is void and considered of no force, unless the person under sixteen received parental permission.[8] When a marriage license is issued, the parties are required to present proof of their age. If you are under eighteen, a special permission form signed by a parent or guardian and notarized is required. Anyone under eighteen but over sixteen must also obtain parental permission to marry in Utah; failure to obtain permission is grounds for an annulment, but will not automatically void a marriage.

After eighteen, men or women in Utah can marry without parental permission.[9]

WHAT ARE THE RESIDENCE REQUIREMENTS FOR A DIVORCE IN UTAH?

A divorce action can be started in any Utah county where either spouse has been a resident for *at least three months* immediately before the filing of the divorce action with the court.

By law, there can be no final court action on the divorce until at least ninety days have passed from the date of the filing of the action. The judge can shorten this period, but usually does not unless there is an extreme situation. Utah divorce laws require this "cooling-off period" in the hope that the couple may reconcile.

After the judge signs the divorce decree and it is noted in court records, it becomes final without any further action by the husband or wife or by the court. There is no longer a waiting period after the divorce is granted before it becomes final.[10]

There are no durational residency requirements or waiting periods for annulments or legal separations, but the person starting the legal action must live in Utah, i.e., be a resident (have an intent to indefinitely continue to live in Utah) for separate maintenance, or a domicile (be living in Utah) for an annulment.

There are no waiting periods for annulments or separate maintenance actions. If someone moved to Utah today, filed an action for an annulment or legal separation tomorrow, and if husband and wife agreed on all terms, the action could be final within weeks.

HOW MUCH WILL A DIVORCE COST IN UTAH?

The average attorney's fee for a simple, uncontested divorce in Utah is between $125 and $400. In addition there are court costs, i.e., filing fees ($77), and sheriff's fees (usually between $25 and $35).

In an uncontested simple divorce, the only court costs are the filing fee. If it is really uncontested, the papers will just be mailed. Thus the only costs will be the filing fee of $77 (in 1986).

If a spouse decides to fight or contest a divorce and goes through a full trial, the attorney's fees will increase and will probably be charged on an hourly basis. Hourly fees vary widely but will probably fall between $50 and $125 per hour. A young attorney will work at $50 to $60 just to keep busy while a seasoned veteran will charge $100-plus per hour. If the divorce is contested, both sides will have to pay similar attorney's fees.

Utah law says that if either spouse cannot afford an attorney in a divorce action, he/she may ask the judge to order the other spouse to pay the attorney's fees, along with the court costs.

CAN MY HUSBAND STOP ME FROM GETTING A DIVORCE?

No, one spouse cannot prevent the other from getting a divorce. But your husband can slow the process down. When someone fights (or contests) a divorce, the disagreements usually involve finances, support, custody of children, or property division. Usually both spouses agree that there should be a divorce but disagree on its terms. By contesting the divorce, the defendant does not prevent it but simply prolongs the process. In Utah, a contested divorce will usually take much longer than the usual three months of an uncontested divorce. It will be at a minimum of three months, and could be more than a year, because of the need for "discovery" and the court's crowded calendar.

WHAT IF MY HUSBAND WON'T ACCEPT THE DIVORCE PAPERS?

Your husband does not have to sign and agree to the terms of the divorce complaint for the divorce to proceed. If he will not voluntarily receive a copy of the complaint and file an answer with the court or other response, then he can be served formally by a sheriff or constable. Upon formal service, if the defendant does not respond within twenty days (file an answer or other legal written response with the clerk of the court), he loses and you are granted (or given) everything you asked for in the complaint. Thus, a divorce can proceed even if the defendant will not cooperate by responding to the papers after being informally (by mail, etc.) served.

WHAT HAPPENS IF THE DEFENDANT DOES NOT RESPOND IN ANY WAY TO THE DIVORCE PAPERS?

If your husband receives the divorce complaint and summons through formal service but does not file any papers to fight or answer them, the divorce will be granted exactly as you ask. The judge will usually not question the reasonable division of property, custody, child support or alimony in your divorce complaint unless there is a response of some sort from the defendant.

If a spouse feels there are errors or unfair requests in the divorce complaint, then he should answer or challenge those items.

After a divorce has been granted, it is difficult to change the terms. If you want to argue about any part of the divorce, it is best to do it when the divorce action is still in process. To change something later, the defending spouse must show a *substantial* change in circumstances.

Even though it may seem difficult to hire a lawyer, the lawyer can best protect your interests when the divorce action is still in process, rather than after the divorce has been granted.

IF MY HUSBAND DOES NOT LIVE IN UTAH, CAN I GET A DIVORCE HERE?

The key to where a divorce can be granted is *jurisdiction*. Jurisdiction simply means that the court has power over the case. Utah law says that if there is a "substantial connection" between the parties, the marriage, and the state of Utah, and the other spouse has been informed in writing about the proceedings, then a Utah court can grant a divorce.

"Substantial connection" means that the parties lived together in Utah during the marriage or that the acts constituting the grounds occurred in Utah—for example, that your husband beat and abandoned you while the two of you were passing through Utah. You should ask an attorney for an answer for your individual case.

If you're a resident of Utah and your husband has never been in Utah, the Utah court can grant a divorce and award custody of children in Utah, but it *cannot* order him to pay child support, alimony, or attorney's fees, or divide the property acquired during the marriage unless he agrees.

CAN I GET A DIVORCE EVEN IF I DON'T KNOW WHERE MY HUSBAND IS LIVING?

You can get a divorce even though your husband cannot be found. If, after you make a diligent search, you cannot find him so he can be personally served with divorce papers, the court will go ahead with the divorce action by giving permission to publish notice of the divorce action in a newspaper and/or to mail notice to the spouse's last known address or to the address of relatives. A divorce granted in this way is restricted to terminating the marriage, granting custody of the children who are in Utah, and dividing property in Utah. The court cannot make any decision about property outside Utah, child support, attorney fees, or alimony in a divorce where notice is given by publication or by mail.

DO I HAVE TO ATTEND COUNSELING BEFORE I FILE FOR A DIVORCE?

Under Utah law, the court *may* require some marriage counseling before a divorce is given. The purpose of the counseling is twofold: to see if the marriage can be held together and, if not, to help prepare the wife and husband for their new roles as unmarrieds. Salt Lake County no longer requires counseling.

Getting a divorce is an emotionally taxing experience for most people, especially when children are involved. An attorney can only provide legal advice. A court can only resolve legal matters. Although it is not a legal requirement, you may wish to seek counseling to help you cope with the emotional and psychological aspects of divorce.

You also need to decide who can best help you with the various problems involved in a divorce. When a lawyer is billing you on an hourly rate, it is wise to use him or her for legal matters and to rely on friends, family, or professional counselors for your non-legal, emotional, and supportive needs.

DO I HAVE TO HIRE A LAWYER?

The law says a person can act as his or her own lawyer and represent himself or herself in court. But since legal proceedings are quite specialized, complicated, and detailed, a person without legal training may have a difficult time with the technical procedures of the court. Most people do not know or understand the complexities of the law or all of the consequences of a legal proceeding. However, a person without an attorney can handle her own simple uncontested divorce.

To protect yourself, you should be represented by an attorney or at least thoroughly discuss the matter with an attorney before proceeding on your own. This book makes every effort to be accurate and authoritative, but it cannot provide legal advice or substitute for an attorney.

WHAT ARE INJUNCTIONS AND TEMPORARY RESTRAINING ORDERS? HOW CAN THEY HELP ME?

An injunction is a court order telling a person to do or not do some specific action, such as move out of a house or stop physical violence against you. A temporary restraining order is a kind of injunction or court order sometimes issued as part of a divorce action. A court may grant a temporary restraining order without letting the person it affects know about it until the order is officially delivered by the sheriff. A court will grant a temporary restraining order *only* when there is *immediate and irreparable* harm that will be suffered unless the order is issued and served.

A temporary restraining order stays in effect for only ten days; and within those ten days, the court must have a hearing, or meeting, with both of you and your attorneys, if any, as to whether the temporary restraining order shall continue in effect. This hearing is usually called "a hearing on an order to show cause," which requires the person being restrained to give reasons why the temporary restraining order should not be continued. At that hearing, the defendant has a chance to explain his or her side. The court is reluctant to take long-term action against anyone without letting them have a chance to give their side of the story. If the temporary restraining order is continued in effect it is called a "preliminary injunction." The same kinds of orders (vacate the house, give you custody of the children, pay temporary support, etc.) are found in both temporary restraining orders and preliminary injunctions. A preliminary injunction is for the "pendency" of an action. When the decree is finally granted and the divorce is no longer "pending," a permanent injunction will be granted, for example, "The defendant is permanently enjoined and restrained from coming around the plaintiff at home or her place of employment, from striking, bothering, or harming her in any manner." The permanent injunction replaces the preliminary injunction.

A temporary restraining order should not be confused with a temporary order. A temporary restraining order is granted without notice when immediate and irreparable harm is threatened and is served on your husband.

A temporary order is usually granted after notice to your husband and after a chance for both sides to be heard. It spells out temporary child custody, support, who pays what bills while the divorce is pending, etc.

Temporary orders are not always necessary but are often used when both of you cannot work things out temporarily. Often a husband will refuse to pay bills or support as a means of putting pressure on his wife during the negotiation process. A temporary order makes the arrangements formal and compulsory.

In a simple, uncontested divorce, there is usually no need for a temporary order.

WHAT HAPPENS IF A COURT ORDER IS IGNORED?

If your husband does not obey a temporary restraining order or other temporary or permanent order of the court, then you must begin further legal proceedings to enforce the order. This means that another court hearing will be scheduled and your husband may be cited for contempt of court for failing to follow the court's order. The court may impose such sanctions such as imprisonment for a set time, imprisonment until he complies with the order (for example, "Defendant shall be held in jail until he reveals the whereabouts of the child of the parties"), a fine, or a fine and/or a jail term suspended (held) upon the party's good behavior.

Usually the police and the sheriff's department will not enforce a temporary restraining order or other court order. Only the court can enforce it, and then only after a hearing. A temporary restraining order or other court order will be effective in the long run and when the court enforces it, but it might not provide the assistance and response that you need immediately.

Under the Utah Spouse Abuse Act you can get a temporary restraining order in a domestic matter without filing and pursuing a divorce. It is a complaint that specifies the abuse or attempted abuse, your belief that the abuse will continue, the specific protection you want, and the specific permanent protection you want ordered at the hearing. Every county court clerk has the necessary forms.

WHAT IS A PERMANENT INJUNCTION?

A permanent injunction is a final court order included in the divorce decree which permanently orders a husband or wife to do or not to do something. For example, if your husband has harassed you at work or at home, a part of the divorce decree may "enjoin and restrain" him from such harassment. If this order is violated, he may be found in contempt of court and punished after a full court hearing like those discussed above.

HOW DOES THE JUDGE DECIDE WHO GETS CUSTODY OF THE CHILDREN?

There are no set rules. The judge has the power under the statutes to award custody of children under the age of eighteen in a "just and proper" way. Other key phrases are "as may be equitable" and considering "the best interests of the child." The law says a judge should consider the best interests of each child and the past conduct and demonstrated moral standards of each parent.[11]

The law says that a judge may talk to a child of any age regarding his or her desires as to future custody but those expressed desires are not controlling. Prior statutes set age limits of twelve, later lowered to ten, about when a child might suggest a nonbinding preference to the court.

CAN I LOSE CUSTODY OF MY CHILD BECAUSE I'M GAY?

In child custody hearings, the primary consideration is the child's welfare. In determining the best interests of the child, a court must consider all relevant factors. In a 1980 case, where the wife was a lesbian, the Utah Supreme Court held that sexual preference is not enough in itself to deprive a parent of custody.[12] However, if the parent is exposing a child to or requiring a child to participate in any sexual activity prohibited by law, or doing anything else the court decides is not in the best interest of the child, then his or her custody or visitation rights may be restricted.

WHAT ABOUT JOINT CUSTODY?

Although a divorce decree may grant custody to one parent or the other, the parents by informal agreement, without going back to court, can rearrange or change their custody/visitation program any way they want. Most divorce decrees simply provide for "reasonable visitation" rights (see next section). The reason for that is so that the parties can work out visitation as necessary when their situations change. By the same token, the parties can, by informal agreement, make whatever custody or visitation arrangements they feel are best for them and their children.

Joint child custody is a legal possibility in Utah and it is becoming more common among divorcing parents. Joint custody means that the divorced parents share responsibility for the care, control, and custody of a child under eighteen. Joint custody can take several forms, all of which require the parents to outline a program compatible with their work schedules, living arrangements, finances, and the child's schooling. It can mean the parents alternate custody every week, or month, or every six months. It can mean that one parent retains actual physical custody of the child but both parents jointly make decisions about the child's daily needs and jointly are responsible for the child's well-being.

The court's ultimate goal in any divorce action is to provide for the "best interests of the child." If those interests are best served by a joint custody arrangement of some type, Utah courts will allow such an arrangement. If the divorcing couple are not both willing to work together for the best interest of their child, there cannot be "joint custody" and one parent must be awarded sole custody. Either parent, if unwilling to cooperate, can prevent joint custody.

The dynamics of divorce often prevent joint custody from being a possible solution, although that seems to be changing as more parents who feel the need to divorce see the benefits of a continuing strong, healthy relationship between both mother and child and father and child.

If divorced parents can work together, joint custody arrangements often benefit children and minimize the harm that often occurs to children in divorce.

WHAT ARE REASONABLE VISITATION RIGHTS?

Normally in a divorce, one parent is awarded custody of the child or children and the other is given "reasonable visitation rights." "Reasonable visitation rights" mean whatever the two parents agree upon. If they cannot agree on visiting schedules or arrangements, they can go back into court and have the judge spell out exact times, places, and method for visits.

The judge prefers parents to work out their own visitation schedules, allowing the person with visitation rights as much time as possible without disrupting the family routine. The court will, however, establish a precise visiting schedule if necessary.

HOW LONG IS CHILD SUPPORT PAID?

In Utah, women and men are minors only until they are eighteen years old. Usually a divorce decree says child support must be paid for the minor children, so child support normally stops at age eighteen or when a child leaves home and takes on the responsibilities of an adult. However it is not unusual to find divorce decrees that provide for support to continue until the child completes high school or college. Child support may also be ordered past eighteen and twenty-one for handicapped or disabled children.

Minority can also be lost by marriage or by a determination (usually by the juvenile court) that the child is "emancipated."

A specific decree can spell out the duration of the child support in different situations, requiring it to be paid until the child is twenty-one, or only to age eighteen, or to eighteen unless the child remains a full-time student and then until age twenty-one.

AFTER THE DIVORCE, WHO CLAIMS THE CHILDREN AS DEPENDENTS FOR INCOME TAX PURPOSES?

After 1984, the parent who has custody of a child for the greater part of the year is treated as the parent who provides more than half the child's support and thus is allowed to claim the child as a dependent for federal income tax purposes.

After 1984, a divorced noncustodial parent may claim a child as a dependent for federal income tax purposes only if:

1. The custodial parent signs a written declaration that he or she will not claim the child and the noncustodial parent attaches this written declaration to his or her tax return; or,

2. A pre-1985 divorce decree gives the dependency exemption to the noncustodial parent and he or she provides at least $600 for the child's support during the year.

Child support is not taxable to the receiving party nor deductible to the paying party.

HOW ARE DEBTS AND PROPERTY DIVIDED IN UTAH?

There is no set standard for the division of debts and property in a divorce action. The judge has the power and the duty to make a *"fair"* division of property acquired during the marriage.

Usually each of you can keep all the property you had before the marriage. The judge will usually decide that whoever has custody of the children needs more of the property to adequately care for them. If there is only one car, it usually goes to the person who needs it to go to and from work. Each of the parties will be awarded their own personal property, clothing, belongings, and effects.

In the same way, the standards for dividing the debts and obligations of the marriage is simply a *fair* division. The person best able to pay is usually responsible for the debts. The judge also considers who will benefit from the payment or who has benefited from whatever created that particular debt. This means whoever is awarded the house will usually be required to make the mortgage payments and the person awarded the car or the furniture will probably have to pay for the outstanding debts on those items. Debts for things which benefited the entire family such as food, utilities, clothing, and rent, will usually be the responsibility of the husband, since by custom he is primarily obligated to support the family.

Personal effects are things like your toothbrush, wallet, driver's license, birth certificate, etc. Clearly, you and your husband should be able to divide those up without too much difficulty. You should also make your own division of small items of household property like pots and pans, cook books, etc. It is not a good use of your money to have two attorneys, each getting $75+ per hour using the expensive and cumbersome machinery of the legal system to decide whether wife or husband gets the $2.98 Foley cake pan and the twelve pints of homemade chili sauce.

Yes, the court will resolve such dispute if you can't, but probably no one will be completely satisfied. Having the parties compromise is much better than letting the court do it. Allowing the judge to decide gives up any control either of you might have had.

If you're disagreeing over something valuable and expensive—a store of fine wines, a valuable stamp or coin collection, a valuable art work, antique furniture, an elaborate set of silver, etc., the court will want to establish a value by appraisal, purchase price, or replacement price, and consider the value in dividing up the total assets of the parties.

After a divorce, people find two households are more expensive than one—two rent payments, two phone bills, etc. The division of property and debts, plus child support, alimony, and legal expenses, usually means that both spouses must accept a lower standard of living than they had during the marriage.

WHAT IS ALIMONY?

Alimony is support money for a divorced spouse. Historically only women could receive alimony; now, by law in Utah and most states, a man can receive alimony, especially when he is "dependent," unable to support himself. "Alimony" is "spousal support."

Alimony is a continuation of the marital, moral, and legal obligation to support a spouse, especially a dependent spouse. Alimony automatically ends when the spouse receiving it remarries, because the law presumes that someone else now has the marital, moral, and legal obligation to provide support.

Alimony is nearly always granted to a wife who has remained at home, raised several children during many years of marriage, has not worked outside the home, and was totally dependent on her husband for financial support. Alimony will probably not be awarded in a marriage of short duration with no children, when both spouses work or have the ability to support themselves.

Alimony may also be granted for a short transitional period of time—a couple of years, for instance—so that the dependent spouse can finish school, acquire job skills etc.

"Token alimony" is a small amount of alimony (like one dollar per year) awarded in a divorce decree simply to keep the obligation of support in the court records. If there is no award of alimony in the decree, the spouse probably can never return to court and seek alimony. If "token alimony" is awarded, the spouse can return to court and seek increased alimony when there is a *substantial* change in either spouse's circumstances.

Under most circumstances, alimony is taxable as income to the receiving party and deductible to the paying party.

CAN MY HUSBAND REFUSE TO PAY ALIMONY BECAUSE I'M GAY?

No. The court orders alimony payments based on financial need, not sexual preference.

CAN I DATE BEFORE MY DIVORCE IS FINAL?

It usually takes three months for a divorce to become final. During that time the husband and wife are still legally married and cannot remarry; thus people pending divorce are *not* single people.

If you are still legally married to one person and date another person, your dating might create grounds (legal reasons) for a divorce or grounds for a countersuit in the divorce action. It probably will cause friction between you and your husband. If you date while the divorce is pending, your husband may threaten to use that fact to prevent you from getting custody of any children involved. The court may consider this factor, but dating alone usually would not prevent you from being awarded custody.

But practically speaking, dating while a divorce is pending is not a problem in most cases.

WHAT DOES A DIVORCE DO TO MY WILL AND MY SPOUSE'S WILL?

By law, a divorce nullifies any provisions of a will which devises, bequeaths, or gives the former spouse property. After a divorce, the parties should prepare new wills to prevent problems that may arise when portions of a will are invalidated.

3 Property Rights

IF I AM MARRIED, CAN I MAKE DECISIONS ABOUT MY PROPERTY AS I PLEASE?

The law generally has two categories of property. "Real" property, roughly, is "unmovable" property like land and buildings (hence the term "real estate"), while personal property is "movable," like clothes, jewelry, money, stocks and bonds, etc. If you own property, you have certain legal rights and obligations. If you wish, you may sell, give, or will your property to someone else.

Historically women have been given fewer property rights than men, however, Utah law never has recognized the "common law" idea that married women are incapable of owning their own property.[1] Laws passed in Utah, before it became a state in 1896, denied the traditional "incapacity" of married women to hold property.[2] Utah's constitution provides that any property a woman acquires before or during marriage is part of her own estate and cannot be used without her permission by anyone, even to pay her husband's debts.[3] She can make decisions about what happens to her property "as if she were unmarried."[4] Utah law also gives married women the right to hold separate real and personal property.[5] Further, if a husband acquires possession or control of his wife's property, she has the right to sue him as if they were not married.[6] A spouse, however, can give to or get from the other spouse a written power of attorney that allows her or him to dispose of his or her property.[7]

WHAT ARE THE LIMITATIONS ON A MARRIED WOMAN'S RIGHTS TO PROPERTY SEPARATE FROM HER HUSBAND'S?

Utah law allows any debts that come from "expenses of the family and the education of the children" to be charged against (or paid by) the property of a husband and/or wife.[8]

The rights given to women also are given to men. This means if a husband acquires property with his own money and keeps title to that property in his name, Utah law gives him all rights of ownership to that property, including the rights to sell, bequeath in a will, and to use the value of that property to pay his debts.

WHAT ARE RIGHTS OF DOWER AND CURTESY?

A dower or curtesy interest is the interest one spouse has in one-third of all real property owned by the other at the time of death. Until 1975, Utah law gave a woman dower rights to one-third of all her husband's real and personal property; however, those rights could be exercised only after his death.[9] Utah law still holds that women who were married and whose husbands died before 1975 are entitled to claim one-third of their husband's property.

In 1975, the Utah legislature abolished all dower and curtesy rights[10] and established an elective-share provision which gave a surviving spouse—husband or wife—the right to a certain part of the deceased's property.[11]

WHAT IS THE ELECTIVE SHARE?

In 1975, the Utah legislature gave a widow or widower the right to choose an "elective share" of his or her spouse's estate, which is similar to dower rights, rather than inheriting through the will of the spouse.[12] To be eligible for such a share, you must have been married to someone who considered Utah his or her home.[13]

The elective share statute provides a complicated formula for determining the actual share of the estate to which you are entitled. Basically, it gives you one-third of the estate after funeral expenses and outstanding bills are paid, multiplied by a fraction based on the relationship of the marital property to the estate after bills have been paid. An attorney can help you identify the legal value of the property you shared with your husband and what your legal share is after his death. The details regarding what property can actually be included in your spouse's estate are very complex. A lawyer can help clarify them.

If, after your spouse's death, you think you might want to choose an elective share rather than the property identified in your husband's will, you must obtain legal advice.

WHAT IS A WILL?

A will is a written document in which you declare your wishes for the disposal of your property, both real and personal. A will becomes effective when you die. All property in which you have an interest at your death becomes your "estate." You should prepare a will regardless of how much property or money you have. Otherwise, property that is not automatically disposed of by a contract, such as life insurance, passes to your survivors by an inflexible formula fixed by law. (This process is described below in the section on dying intestate.) Those who are named in a will to receive an inheritance are called heirs.

It is recommended, generally, that you have an attorney prepare your will, because there are certain legal formalities that must be observed for the will to be "probated" after your death. "Probate" is the process by which a will is accepted by a court as the last legal statement of the deceased's intentions for distribution of the estate.

HOW DO I KNOW IF MY WILL IS VALID?

To create a valid will, you must be mentally competent, at least eighteen years old, intend the will to distribute your property at the time of your death, and not be unduly influenced or defrauded by others.

In addition, a formal will must be in writing, signed by you (the "testator"), and signed by at least two "disinterested" witnesses who are at least eighteen.[15] The "witnesses" must watch you sign the will and must sign in the presence of each other. A witness can receive property under the terms of the will and still be disinterested, if he or she receives less than he or she would if you died without making a will. Generally, it is better to get witnesses who do not receive property under the will. If you are unable to sign your will, someone else may sign, but only at your request and direction.[16] It is best to sign at the end of the will so that nothing can be added by another person. Because of differences in state laws, it is better to obtain three witnesses, rather than the two required by Utah law.

Utah law recognizes "holographic" wills, which are in the will maker's handwriting and not witnessed.[17] The old rules said that a holographic will must be entirely in the will maker's handwriting. Utah law now requires that at least the important parts of the will, those that dispose of property, be in the will maker's handwriting.[18]

Oral wills are not recognized as legally valid in Utah. Few states accept such wills as valid.

WHAT DOES A WILL DO?

Your intentions for the disposition of your property, as expressed in your will, will be followed as closely as possible. With few limitations, you may leave your property in any manner and to anyone that you choose. The major exception to this rule is designed to help the surviving spouse. She or he has the option of accepting the share of the estate left by the will, or of renouncing the will and choosing to take the elective share described earlier.[19]

CAN PROPERTY BE TRANSFERRED AT DEATH BY MEANS OTHER THAN A WILL?

Most contracts that are intended to pass property upon death of one of the people involved cannot be legally enforced. Life insurance policies and pension funds, however, will be enforced.

A joint account in your name and the name of another person, including your spouse, which is payable to either person or to the survivor if one dies, will permit the surviving person to keep the money in the account.[20]

You can create an account in your name "in trust" for another person, who is known as a beneficiary.[21] "In trust" simply means that you are giving the money to the beneficiary, but are retaining control over the administration of the funds. After your death, that person may withdraw the money.[22]

Finally, real property (basically land and buildings) can be owned by two people, in what is called joint tenancy. Joint tenancy means that if one person dies, the surviving owner owns the entire property. Joint tenants need not be married.

WHAT DOES "INTESTATE" MEAN?

When you die without leaving a will, you die "intestate," literally, without a legal will or testament. The intestate estate is the total property of the person who died without a will, except property that is transferred by insurance contract, joint account, trust, or joint tenancy.

Utah law specifically describes which relatives will inherit what property if someone dies without a legal will.

IF MY HUSBAND DIES INTESTATE, WHAT DO I INHERIT?

Your inheritance depends on the circumstances. If there are no surviving children or parents of your dead spouse, the entire intestate estate is yours. If there are no surviving children of your spouse but his parents are still alive, the first $100,000, plus one-half of the balance of the intestate estate belongs to you. If there are surviving children who are also your children, the first $50,000, plus one-half of the balance of the intestate estate is yours. If there are surviving children but one or more of them are not your children, you inherit one-half of the intestate estate.[23]

WHAT IF I AM A LEGAL HEIR OF SOMEONE WHO DIES INTESTATE?

If a woman is an heir of someone who dies intestate, she receives a portion of the estate only after other claims have been paid. Utah law states that intestate property first passes to the dead person's children "by representation," meaning that they take equal shares with each person related to the deceased in the same degree of kinship. For example, brothers and sisters take equal shares. If there are no surviving children, property passes equally to the dead person's living parents. If there are no living children or parents of the deceased, property passes to the parents' children by representation. If there are no surviving children, parents or parents' children, and there are surviving grandparents or grandparents' children, half of the property goes to the paternal grandparents (that is the deceased's father's parents) or to their children by representation if the grandparents died before the decedent. The other half passes to the maternal relatives (that is, those related to the deceased's mother's parents) in the same way. If only one family side is surviving, all property passes to that side.

If there are no surviving children, parents, parents' children, grandparents, or grandparents' children, the property passes to the next of kin in equal degree.[24]

ARE THERE OTHER QUALIFICATIONS TO INHERIT PART OF THE INTESTATE ESTATE?

Utah law says that any heir receiving property through intestacy—that is, without a legal will—must survive the decedent by 120 hours.[25] Also, the decedent's relatives of half blood inherit as if they were of whole blood.[26] A "half blood" relative is related to the deceased by only one common ancestor, rather than two; for example, you are a child of the deceased's mother but not of the deceased's father. In addition, relatives of the decedent who were conceived before, but born after death, inherit as if they had been born at the time the decedent died.[27] It does not matter if the heir, or the person whom the heir inherits through, is an alien or a citizen of the United States.[28]

For purposes of intestate succession, an adopted person is considered to be the biological child of the adopting parents.[29] An illegitimate child is considered a child of the mother only; unless the parents were married at the time of birth, but the marriage was later declared void, or paternity (fatherhood) is established by a court.[30] Generally, fatherhood must be legally established before death. The requirements to obtain a declaration of paternity after death are much more strict. Accordingly, steps should be taken before death to have a court issue a declaration of paternity.

BEFORE I MARRY, CAN I ENTER INTO AN AGREEMENT WITH MY FUTURE HUSBAND ABOUT OWNERSHIP OF PROPERTY?

Yes. An agreement that you make with your prospective spouse is called a prenuptial or antenuptial agreement. There are many reasons for such an agreement. First, it makes you talk about each person's assets and liabilities. In fact, it is essential that both of you know and understand the extent of property, debts, and income of the other to obtain a valid prenuptial agreement. Second, you may wish to retain separate property after the marriage and later decide to give that property to someone other than your spouse. In an antenuptial agreement, your future husband can renounce or deny any claim to that property. Third, you could obtain a position where you earn more money than your husband. If this happens and you later divorce, the law may require you to pay alimony to your husband. Either a husband or wife can waive any claim to alimony in a prenuptial agreement.

A valid prenuptial agreement must meet certain requirements. Both people must have completely disclosed their assets and liabilities. The agreement must be in writing and signed by each person, and the signatures should be notarized. Neither person can be subjected to undue influence—that is, can be forced, threatened, or bribed to sign the document. If the value, extent, or ownership of property has been misrepresented, the agreement could be rendered void.[31]

When you think about preparing a prenuptial agreement, you should be absolutely certain that your intended husband is being completely honest in his disclosures. You should not sign the agreement until you understand all of its terms and conditions. An antenuptial agreement is a very important document. If you have any questions, do not hesitate to seek advice from a third party, preferably an attorney.

4 Money Problems and Bankruptcy

WHAT IS BANKRUPTCY?

Bankruptcy has two meanings. In common speech, we say someone is bankrupt when she is overburdened by her financial obligations and cannot pay all of her bills. Bankruptcy as a legal state is a court's declaration that you cannot pay and cannot be held accountable to your creditors except through the court.

The Federal Bankruptcy Code[1] is designed to help individuals, partnerships, or corporations who can no longer meet their financial obligations.

HOW DOES BANKRUPTCY AFFECT ME?

Bankruptcy laws can affect you in various ways. You might find yourself in a position where you cannot pay your bills or make loan or mortgage payments. Or a person, partnership, or corporation who owes *you* money files for relief under the Bankruptcy Code and you receive notice from the court of the bankruptcy proceedings.

Before taking any action on the information contained in this chapter, please consult an attorney who is experienced in bankruptcy law. A lawyer can give you more specific and individualized assistance about your alternatives whether you owe money or whether someone owes you money. Even if you feel you cannot afford an attorney's services, you should at least seek a consultation with one to explain the law to you. The Utah State Bar's Lawyer Referral Office (531-9075) will refer you to a lawyer who will meet with you for $15 for the first thirty-minute visit. The Legal Aid Society or a private attorney can also arrange a referral for such a consultation.

AM I A CREDITOR?

You are a "creditor"[2] of a "debtor"[3] (someone in debt to you) under the Bankruptcy Code when you have a "claim,"[4] or a right to payment from someone who has declared bankruptcy.

Often the first time you learn that someone who owes you money has filed bankruptcy will be when you receive in the mail a document called "Order for Relief and Notice of First Meeting of Creditors." The person who owes you money is required to list the names and addresses of all his or her creditors so that they can be given written notice. When bankruptcy papers are filed, an "automatic stay"[5] goes into effect which stops, among other things, all efforts to collect money owed.

You can go to the first meeting of creditors, ask the debtor questions, and hear what the debtor, his or her attorney, and the trustee have to say about how the case will proceed. The trustee is chosen by the Bankruptcy Court from a panel of trustees. He or she is an officer of the court, not an attorney for any side. His or her name is always given on the "Order for Relief."

If you are a creditor of someone you discover has filed a bankruptcy and you have not received any notice in the mail, you should immediately go to the clerk of the Bankruptcy Court. In Salt Lake City it is in Room 361, U.S. Courthouse and Post Office at 350 South Main Street. Look at the debtor's file to see if (or how) you are listed as a creditor, and contact an attorney for advice about your legal rights and remedies.

WHAT CAN I DO TO GET MY MONEY FROM SOMEONE WHO DECLARES BANKRUPTCY?

If someone owes you money, you will want to do everything you can to legally protect and collect your claim. This is the reason you should consult an attorney who is knowledgeable in bankruptcy law.

The person who owes money can request relief under the Bankruptcy Code in several different ways. (See below, "WHAT TYPES OF PROCEEDINGS ARE PROVIDED FOR BY THE CODE?") Generally, your rights and remedies under the code depend on the type of proceedings the debtor chooses.

In most cases, in order to protect your claim you or your attorney should quickly file a Proof of Claim in the debtor's case. In the Proof of Claim, you explain the reason the debtor owes you money, what that amount is, and identify any lien[6] or security[7] for your claim.

A lien or security is usually "real property" such as land and buildings, or "personal property," such as cars, jewelry, or furniture. Another word for *lien* or *security* is *collateral*. If you have a lien or security for your claim, you may, in some situations get authorization from the Bankruptcy Court to get your property back from the debtor in exchange for giving up part or all of your claim. Again, please hire an attorney to do this for you as the required proceedings are very technical and often complex.

If you are the landlord of a debtor, you have a right to collect ongoing rents from the debtor which become due after the date his bankruptcy was filed. Again, since the procedures for accomplishing this are technical, you should immediately consult an attorney.

To best protect your claim against the debtor, *don't delay*. You should promptly consult an attorney, file a Proof of Claim, and keep informed of the progress of the case. Most bankruptcy cases are resolved quickly, within three to six months after the first filing. Others, depending on their complexity, can take much longer. In almost every case, interested creditors can help move the case along.

WILL I GET MY MONEY BACK FROM A DEBTOR WHO DECLARES BANKRUPTCY?

Whether you will get your money back from a debtor who declares bankruptcy depends on what kind of a claim you have. For example, if the bankruptcy is a Chapter 7 (these types are explained later in the chapter), unsecured creditors get paid nothing if the court determines that there are no assets from which creditors may be paid. If it is a Chapter 11 or a Chapter 13 bankruptcy and the person owes you wages, you'll be paid first. If you have a secured claim, you'll either be paid the presently determined fair value for the item through the plan or you'll get the security back. For instance, if you sold a car to X who subsequently declared bankruptcy and still owes you $1,500 on the car worth $1,000, you'll either get paid $1,000 through the plan or you'll get the car back. If the debtor keeps the car and pays $1,000, your claim for $500 goes into a pot with all the other claims and you'll be paid according to what proportion of the whole amount your $500 is (pro rata).

WHAT SHOULD I KNOW IF I BECOME A DEBTOR?

If you find that you cannot pay your bills and your creditors are pressuring you, you may wish to consider one of the kinds of debt relief provided by the Bankruptcy Code and give yourself a chance for a fresh start.

You should know that there are some alternatives to declaring bankruptcy. You could work out an arrangement with individual creditors to pay in certain installments. However, if you have signed a note agreeing to pay $150 on some furniture by the 15th of each month, it may not matter that you work out an arrangement to pay $75 for twice as long. If the creditor chooses, he or she can legally sue on the basis of the written document. The alternative arrangement will not be legally binding unless you also put it into writing.

If a creditor won't negotiate with you or make some arrangement for payment, you could consult a credit counseling service listed in the yellow pages. Their services are sometimes helpful in explaining different options to you and sometimes helping you work out arrangements with creditors. Under the state law, you and your creditors can voluntarily agree to a repayment plan with the same terms as a court-ordered "reorganization" (Chapter 11) or Chapter 13 Plan. However, if only one creditor refuses to go along with this arrangement, it isn't binding on any of them and you have to go to court. (It's impossible to work out this kind of arrangement without a lawyer; the state statute is very complicated.)

Even though the great advantage of bankruptcy is that it lets you start over again with a clean slate, there are some disadvantages that make repayment arrangements worth considering. Your reputation suffers and the declaration of bankruptcy will be reported on your credit history. You can only file bankruptcy every six years, so it's not a cheap or easy way to get yourself out of a minor financial hole.

WHAT TYPES OF PROCEDURES DOES THE BANKRUPTCY CODE PROVIDE?

Bankruptcy proceedings may be either voluntary or involuntary. "Voluntary" means that you have taken the initiative yourself to seek this form of relief. In contrast, your creditors begin an "involuntary" proceeding. This usually happens only when debts are connected to a business. Few creditors launch bankruptcy proceedings to collect personal accounts.

You can be subjected to a great deal of pressure, however, when you owe someone money. If someone has lent you money on your car or your furniture, they can take them away from you. They can take you to court directly or refer the case to a collection agency who will sue you in a state court for a percentage of the money owed. If the sum is small enough, they can take you to a small claims court. If you ran up the debt on a credit card, your bank or the store can cancel your credit with them.

There are, however, some restrictions on what a creditor or collection agency can do. They are not allowed to call you at the office if you ask them not to and they cannot call during normal sleeping hours. They also cannot exaggerate the legal consequences of what will happen to you if you don't pay.

The Bankruptcy Code offers various types of proceedings. One is a Chapter 7 liquidation proceeding ("Chapter" refers to part of the code). This process authorizes the Trustee to gather together all your nonexempt assets and sell them, or "liquidate" them to cash. ("Exempt" assets are those which cannot be reached by your creditors.)[8] In Utah, the exemptions you may claim in bankruptcy are provided by state law.[9]

When you talk to an attorney, he or she will tell you about the list of exempt items. The list of items includes some furniture, basic household appliances like a refrigerator, washer and dryer, clothing, and sometimes some heirlooms. The statute also specifies dollar amounts of the exemptions. If you use a car in your business or profession, it is exempt up to $1,500. Driving back and forth to work is considered personal use, not professional use. A plumber's truck would be considered professional. The tools of your trade are exempt up to $1,500. You can keep $500 worth of furniture, $500 worth of animals, books, and musical instruments, and $500 worth of heirlooms or sentimental items.

The statute also specifies a "right of homestead," or the right of a person to live in a house and have a value retained in that house. A head of house can have a value of $8,000 in a house, a spouse can have $2,000, and $500 can be claimed for each dependent. If you have a mortgage on the house, the homestead right does not apply except on the equity. If your house is worth $50,000 and you have a first mortgage of $20,000, you would deduct the homestead allowance from the $30,000 difference or equity. Alimony, support, and maintenance are also exempt from claims of creditors. See the State Exemption Statute, for the complete list.

If the Trustee decides to liquidate your nonexempt assets, the cash will be distributed among your unsecured creditors (those who do not have a lien or security) on a pro-rata basis. That is, each creditor will receive an amount of cash proportionate to the size of that creditor's claim against you. If your only assets are exempt or of nominal value, the trustee will probably close your case as a "no-asset" case, and your creditors will receive nothing on their claims. A Chapter 7 liquidation proceeding may be either voluntary or involuntary.

Another alternative provided by the code is known as a Chapter 13 or "Adjustment of Debts of an Individual with Regular Income." Basically, this method allows someone with regular income (such as wages or any form of government payments or assistance) to work out a plan to pay off her outstanding debts, in full or in part, over a specified period of time no longer than sixty months. A bankruptcy judge must "confirm" the plan before it goes into effect.

Chapter 13 can solve the problem of curing delinquencies in your mortgage and other secured debts along with your unsecured debts. Most mortgages and secured debts provide for foreclosure and repossession if you fall behind on your monthly payments. Chapter 13 would allow you to make the current payments and make up the delinquencies (cure the default) over the time of the plan without fear of foreclosure or repossession.

Once the plan has been confirmed by the Bankruptcy Judge, the creditors have no choice. They have to accept it and so do you. If you don't pay on schedule, the standing trustee files a motion. The motion will ask that your matter be converted to a Chapter 7 (see the above section), or that it be dismissed. If it is dismissed, then it's a race to the courthouse for the creditors since the first one with a judgment against you can get your nonexempt property.

Note that you are the only one who can file a Chapter 13; your creditors cannot force you to accept such a plan. You also have a right to "convert" this proceeding into a Chapter 7 liquidation bankruptcy at any point, but your creditors can't convert it unless you default.

The code also provides for a Chapter 11, "Reorganization of Debt," proceeding. This chapter is most commonly used by businesses (corporations or partnerships) and allows the business to remain in operation. The debtor proposes a payment plan for her creditors, which must be confirmed by the bankruptcy judge after creditors have had a chance to vote for or against it.

WHAT IS THE PROCEDURE FOR VOLUNTARY FILING?

You must file a petition with the Bankruptcy Court and pay a $60 fee for either a Chapter 7 or a Chapter 13. The fee for a Chapter 11 is $200. Payment of this fee is mandatory, but under some circumstances it may be paid in installments.

You and your husband may decide to file a joint case[10] if you are both responsible for your debts and own most of your property together. This procedure is designed to reduce legal and court costs and allow a speedier decision. Under this procedure you are required to pay only one filing fee.

After your petition has been filed, the court will issue an "Order for Relief" and the "automatic stay" described above goes into effect. This means that all collection efforts, harassment, and lawsuits against you cease immediately. This gives you a breathing spell from your creditors' attempts to collect from you. In a Chapter 13 proceeding, the "automatic stay" provision also protects your codebtors who have not filed petitions in bankruptcy.[11] For example, for nonbusiness debts like personal items, family expenses, or household expenses where someone cosigns with you, then until the creditor files a request with the court for permission to pursue the cosigner, Chapter 13 protects the cosigner against the creditor too. Cosigning on a business loan would not be protected. Consumer debts also include charge-card expenses for a vacation, a restaurant bill, clothes, etc.

WHAT HAPPENS TO ME, MY ASSETS, AND MY DEBTS IF I CHOOSE A CHAPTER 7?

If you choose a Chapter 7 liquidation bankruptcy, a Trustee is appointed by the court to "collect" your assets under the supervision of a bankruptcy judge. The trustee has the right to inventory and evaluate all of your property to see if it may be used to pay your debts. But you are permitted to claim certain property as "exempt," or beyond the reach of your creditors.

Once your nonexempt assets (if any) have been collected, "liquidated," and the cash from the sale distributed among your creditors, (or if the trustee decides yours is a "no-asset" case), you will usually be granted a "discharge"[12] of your outstanding debts and have no legal obligation to pay them. There are, however, a few important exceptions.[13] A divorced spouse who declares bankruptcy must still pay alimony or child support if he or she had that obligation. You must still pay some other types of obligations, like debts you acquire through false pretenses or the use of a false written statement[14] or certain taxes.[15]

The "discharge" is designed to give you a fresh start. In effect, the slate is wiped clean of your past debts.[16] To encourage the fresh start, the code says no government office can discriminate against you just because you have gone through a bankruptcy proceeding. This means you cannot lose your job whether with the government or private industry, or be denied a driver's license or other license solely because of your bankruptcy.[17]

WHAT'S A REAFFIRMATION?

Even though you have "discharge" and opportunity for a new beginning, you may decide to "reaffirm" your legal obligation to pay a particular debt.[18] You make this decision for a variety of reasons. If the "reaffirmation" involves a consumer debt—as for a TV from a department store—the reaffirmation agreement must be in writing, signed by the creditor, you, and your attorney, and filed with the Court before your discharge is granted. Only after you take all these steps will you be legally required to pay that particular debt as though the discharge had never occurred. Of course, you may decide to voluntarily pay some or all of the debts from which you are discharged, but you're not legally obligated to do so and your creditors cannot require you to do so.

Reaffirming is completely voluntary on the debtor's part. If you are a creditor and there's a possibility of reaffirmation, our advice to you is to get the best lawyer you can afford.

WHAT IF I DECIDE TO TRY A CHAPTER 13?

As discussed earlier, the Chapter 7 liquidation is just one of your alternatives. You may decide to use the Chapter 13 proceeding. If you choose this alternative, you will not have to be concerned about the question of exemptions and you will be allowed to keep your property and pay your debts through the plan you work out with the trustee and your creditors. In many cases, the bankruptcy court will simply order your employer to make a payroll deduction from your wages of the amount required in the "confirmed" Chapter 13 plan. That amount goes directly to the Chapter 13 trustee who will send payments to your creditors according to your individual plan.

After all payments provided by your Chapter 13 plan have been made (over a period of time no longer than sixty months), you will receive a "discharge" from all debts included in the plan.[19] This gives you a clean slate except for obligations for alimony, child support, and mortgage or other secured obligations. Under a Chapter 11 or 7 bankruptcy, there are some additional exceptions from discharge. There you are still liable—quite understandably—for taxes, debt incurred through false pretenses, embezzlement, torts (a fine you've been ordered to pay for beating someone up, for instance), and student loans. If you are not able to perform according to your plan because of "hardship" (for example, you lose your job or get sick), the court could grant you the same discharge you would receive under Chapter 7.

WHAT EFFECT WILL BANKRUPTCY HAVE ON MY ABILITY TO OBTAIN CREDIT?

Ironically, you may be viewed by some creditors as a good credit risk once you have gone through the proceeding. This is because the code says that you may not be granted another "discharge" of debts for at least six years.[20] Other creditors, however, may be reluctant to give you credit and may, in fact, lawfully refuse you credit because of your previous record. The fact of your bankruptcy may remain a part of your credit history for as long as fourteen years under the terms of the Fair Credit Reporting Act. As a result, you may experience difficulty in getting credit except where high rates of interest are charged. This is a significant result of bankruptcy and one you should think about carefully before you decide to file a petition.

CAN A CREDITOR DENY ME CREDIT BECAUSE OF MY HUSBAND'S BANKRUPTCY?

If you did not file a joint bankruptcy petition with your husband and you are applying for an unsecured loan which you alone are responsible for repaying, a creditor may not legally deny you the loan because of your husband's bankruptcy. To do so violates the Equal Credit Opportunity Act.

HOW MUCH WILL IT COST ME TO FILE BANKRUPTCY?

First there are the filing fees: $60 for a joint petition under Chapters 7 and 13. A Chapter 11 reorganization fee is $200. Legal fees will be on top of that. Attorneys generally charge for services based upon their respective hourly rates. The total fee depends on the complexity of the case. In Chapter 7 cases, you usually have to pay the fees immediately. If you file a Chapter 13 bankruptcy, you can sometimes pay part of it and negotiate an arrangement to have the rest paid in installments out of your monthly payments along with the other creditors. In all cases, the fees have to be approved by the court. You must usually give your attorney a retainer when you employ his or her services. This retainer will be disclosed to the court; final fees are submitted to and approved by the court before payment.

5 Taxes

NOTE: Most of this chapter represents current tax law as of August, 1986. Because of major revisions that were and are being considered by the U.S. Congress, the reader is advised to contact an attorney, accountant, or other tax consultant about specific issues of concern.

WHAT DOES BEING A WOMAN HAVE TO DO WITH TAXES?

It's not being a woman—it's being a *married* woman. Tax laws, whether federal, state, or local are generally written in sex-neutral terms[1] except when it comes to marital status and employment status.[2] As a woman taxpayer, you should know the ways in which your marital status or a change in your marital status may change your tax liability (meaning the taxes you are required to pay).

This chapter discusses federal income, estate, and gift tax law. Some of the tax provisions are relatively new. Where significant, the difference between the old law and the new law have been explained and the dates on which the changes are effective have been included.

INCOME TAXES

HOW DOES MY MARITAL STATUS AFFECT THE AMOUNT OF FEDERAL INCOME TAX I PAY?

Your filing status (or the tax class you fit into) is pretty much determined by your marital status. It determines the particular set of tax rates that will be applied to your income and, in some instances, affects your eligibility for certain exemptions, deductions, and credits.

Your filing status also determines your "zero bracket amount," which is the maximum amount of income you may receive in a year without having to pay income taxes. Here's a list of those status differences. The explanations of the terms comes in the next question and answer.

Filing Status	Zero Bracket Amounts for 1985 Tax Year
Married-joint return	$3,540
Married-separate return	$1,770
Single (including divorced)	$2,390
Certain Widows or Widowers ("Surviving Spouse")	$3,540
Head of Household	$2,390

HOW DO I DETERMINE MY FILING STATUS?

Your filing status is determined on the last day of the year for which you are filing a tax return.[3]

You qualify as "single" for federal income tax purposes if you file an individual or separate return, and:

1. You have never been married;
2. You are a widow whose husband died more than two years before the year in question;
3. You have obtained a final decree of divorce or separate maintenance on or before the last day of the year; or
4. You have obtained a decree of annulment. If you had claimed married status for any of the last three years, due to your now-annulled marriage, then you must also file amended returns claiming single status for those years. This is required because a decree of annulment declares that no valid marriage existed.[4]

If you are single, you may also qualify as a "head of household"[5] giving you a lower tax class than "single" if:

1. You are unmarried on the last day of the tax year; and
2. You paid for more than half the maintenance of your home; and
3. Your home is the principal residence of yourself, your children, or another dependent relative, like a sister or mother in need of support.

You are considered "married"[6] for federal tax purposes if, on the last day of the tax year:

1. You are actually married and living with your husband;
2. You are not living together but are not legally separated under a decree of divorce or separate maintenance; or
3. You and your husband are separated under an interlocutory decree of divorce, waiting for the divorce to be final.

The IRS lets common-law marriages determine your federal income-tax filing status[7] if the state you are living in recognizes common-law marriages. Utah does not, however, if you and your husband have a valid common law marriage as defined by the laws of the state in which you were living, and then move to Utah, Utah must also recognize that marriage as valid. For example, in Denver you will be recognized as married if you cohabitate and repute to be married, i.e., refer to yourself as Mrs. John Doe.

If you and your husband file a joint return, the applicable tax rates will, in effect, split your combined income. This is an advantage if one of you makes significantly more than the other, since your combined incomes are taxed as though you each made half.

If your husband died during the year, you are deemed a "surviving spouse" and may file a joint return for that year[8] if you wish—usually a tax break. You can still get income-splitting benefits for the next two years (a total of three years altogether) if:

1. You were eligible to file a joint return the year your spouse died;
2. A dependent child, stepchild, or foster child lived with you for the year;
3. You paid over half the household expenses; and
4. You have not remarried by the end of the tax year.

If you are a serviceman's widow, and he is missing in action, you may claim this "surviving spouse" status for the two years following the declaration of death rather than actual death.[9]

If you remarry before the end of the tax year in which your spouse died, you cannot file a joint return as the "surviving spouse" of your deceased husband, but you may, of course, file jointly with your new husband.

WHAT ARE THE ADVANTAGES AND DISADVANTAGES OF FILING A JOINT RETURN?

We've already mentioned the most important one: the tax rates are generally lower than they would be if you filed separately. In some cases, however, filing separately may result in less tax. For example, the deduction for medical expenses is allowed only to the extent that those expenses exceed 5 percent of adjusted gross income. If you have a moderate income and substantial medical expenses while your husband has few or no medical expenses, you could take a larger medical expenses deduction if you file separately. In any event, you should always calculate your taxes both ways to see which way will minimize your combined tax burden.

If either you or your husband receives federal or state unemployment compensation or certain disability payments, recent change in the tax laws may make it worthwhile to file separately. The 1978 Revenue Act overturned a series of IRS rulings that said government-paid unemployment benefits are not tax-exempt. Beginning in 1979, they have been taxed when they exceed a "base amount exemption." This exemption for 1985 is $12,000 for single individuals, $18,000 married couples filing jointly, zero for couples filing separately, and $12,000 for married couples not filing a joint return who did not live with a spouse at any time during the year.[10]

Some additional tax benefits are also not available to married couples unless they file a joint return. These include the child care and dependent care credit as well as the earned income credit, tax credit for the elderly, and deductions for working couples, all discussed later.

A disadvantage to the joint return is that you and your husband are not only jointly liable for the tax; but if your husband dies, disappears, or is incarcerated each of you is separately liable for the entire tax.[11] The so-called "Innocent Spouse Provision"[12] in the tax code will relieve you from liability on a joint return in these fairly limited circumstances:

1. If your spouse has omitted funds from the gross income reported jointly that exceed 25 percent of the total reported, *and*
2. If you can prove that you not only did not know about this omission but had no reason to know of it; and
3. If it would be inequitable to hold you liable for the tax deficiency in light of the circumstances.

HAVE YOU HEARD ABOUT A DEDUCTION FOR WORKING COUPLES?

Yes. For quite a few years, when both a husband and wife worked, they paid higher taxes on their joint income than they would have by filing returns as single taxpayers.

In 1981, Congress passed the Economic Recovery Tax Act giving an important new tax break to a married couple when both work and file a joint return. 1983 was the second year married taxpayers have been able to take this deduction.

For 1982, the deduction was limited to 5 percent of the qualified earned income of the lesser-earning spouse, up to $30,000, for a maximum deduction of $1,500. In 1983 and 1984, the deduction was even more valuable. You could deduct the smaller of 10 percent of the qualified earned income of the lesser-earning spouse or 10 percent of$30,000, whichever was smaller, for a maximum deduction of $3,000. If you qualified for this deduction in either 1982, 1983, 1984, and/or 1985 you can still take it by filing an amended return, using Form 1040X.

Since the deduction is used to figure adjusted gross income, it's not necessary to itemize deductions, which means that taxpayers may use Form 1040A.

Not all income qualifies for this deduction. The income must be earned income—wages, salaries, tips, etc. Income one spouse pays another does not qualify. You also can't count income from interest, dividends, pensions, annuities, distributions from an individual retirement arrangement (IRA), unemployment compensation, deferred compensation, or nontaxable income. In addition, after you determine your earned income, you have to make certain adjustments to arrive at qualified earned income—the amount actually used to figure the deduction. For example, you have to reduce your income by the amount you paid to an IRA, you can't count employee business expenses, and you can't count the disability income exclusion.

If you file Form 2555, "Foreign Earned Income," to exclude any income from tax or to deduct certain housing costs or if you file Form 4563, "Exclusion of Income from Sources in United States Possessions," to exclude income from tax, you may not take the deduction.

Community property laws do not apply when determining qualified earned income. That is, the income is treated as the separate income of the spouse who earns it, rather than community income.

HOW DOES MY MARITAL STATUS AFFECT THE NUMBER OF EXEMPTIONS I AM ALLOWED?

The personal exemptions provision means you can exclude a flat amount from your income. Beginning in 1985 that amount is $1,040 per exemption. You can have one personal exemption for yourself, your spouse, each dependent, and the blindness of yourself and/or your spouse. You may also claim an additional exemption if you or your husband are over sixty-five.

If you are married, or separated but not under a final divorce decree, or were widowed during the tax year, and you file a joint return, then you may claim two exemptions—one for yourself and one for your husband.[13] If you but not your husband file a separate return, you may claim an exemption for your husband too if he had no income and was not someone else's dependent. If you and your husband file separately, then you may only take your own exemption deductions.

If you are divorced or separated, you should be aware of the special rules that apply to dependency exemptions for children of divorced or separated parents.[14]

After 1984, the parent who has custody of a child for the greater part of the year is generally treated as the parent who provides more than half the child's support and thus is allowed to claim the child as a dependent for federal income tax purposes.

After 1984, a divorced noncustodial parent may claim a child as a dependent for federal income tax purposes only if:

1. The custodial parent signs a written declaration that he or she will not claim the child and the noncustodial parent attaches this written declaration to his or her tax return; or,
2. A pre-1985 divorce decree gives the dependency exemption to the noncustodial parent and he or she provides at least $600 for the child's support during the year.

Child support is not taxable to the receiving party nor deductible to the paying party. Where the issue of support is contested, each parent must submit itemized statements of what was actually spent. This places a burden upon the custodial parent (very often the woman) to keep accurate records of expenditures. If you have remarried, support provided by your new spouse is considered with your contribution.[15]

It is important to remember that once you establish your right to a dependency exemption for your child under these rules, you are also eligible for a child-care credit for the child.

WHAT DEDUCTIONS AND CREDITS ARE PARTICULARLY IMPORTANT TO ME AS A WOMAN TAXPAYER?

Certain deductions especially important to women include those allowed for divorce expenses and medical expenses.

During the course of a divorce, you may deduct fees charged by either a lawyer or an accountant for tax advice, but not deduct legal fees for representation in the divorce.[16] If you have to sue to get or collect alimony, you may be able to deduct these fees as income-producing expenses.[17] You can deduct alimony that you pay,[18] assuming the wife pays alimony and doesn't have custody of the children, but no deductions are allowed for any property transferred as a result of the divorce. *If you are the noncustodial parent,* you do not get a deduction for child support payments.[19]

Deductions are allowed for such medical expenses as contraceptives prescribed by your doctor,[20] legal abortions,[21] and voluntary sterilizations.[22] Care of a normal and healthy baby by a nurse, diaper services, etc., do not qualify as deductible medical expenses.[23] If your insurance paid for the expense or you were otherwise reimbursed, you cannot take the deduction. Medical deductions are subject to certain limitations that are explained on your tax forms, and in further detail in "Deduction for Medical and Dental Expenses," Publication 502 of the Internal Revenue Service.

An important tax break for many working women is the Child Care and Disabled Dependent Care Credit.[24] If you are responsible for dependent care expenses, you may qualify for the Child Care Credit. The expenses you incur must be paid for the care of:

Any person under age 15 whom you claim as a dependent (but see the special rule later for children of divorced or separated parents below).

Your disabled spouse who is mentally or physically unable to care for himself or herself.

Any disabled person who is mentally or physically unable to care for himself or herself and whom you claim as a dependent, or could claim as a dependent except that he or she had income of $1,040 or more.

Children of divorced or separated parents—If you were divorced, legally separated, or lived apart from your spouse during the last 6 months of 1985, you may be able to claim the credit even if your child is not your dependent. If your child is not your dependent, he or she is a qualifying person if *all five* of the following apply:

1. You had custody of the child for the longer period during the year; and
2. The child received over half of his or her support from one or both of the parents; and
3. The child was in the custody of one or both of the parents over half of the year; and
4. The child was under age 15, or was physically or mentally unable to care for himself or herself; and
5. The child is not your dependent because—
   a. As the custodial parent you have signed Form 8332, Release of Claim to Exemption for Child of Divorced or Separated

Parents, or a similar statement, agreeing not to claim the child's exemption for 1985; or

b. You were divorced or separated before 1985 and your divorce decree or written agreement states that the other parent can claim the child's exemption, and the other parent provides at least $600 in child support during the year. (Note: This rule does not apply if your decree or agreement was changed after 1984 to specify that the other parent cannot claim the child's exemption.)

You are eligible for all the credit if all five of the following apply:

1. You paid for the care so you (and your spouse if you were married) could work or look for work (exception to the rules are a spouse who is a full-time student or is disabled). See note below.
2. You and the qualifying person(s) lived in the same home.
3. You (and your spouse if you were married) paid over half the cost of keeping up your home. The cost includes: rent; mortgage interest; property taxes; utilities; home repairs; and food eaten at home.
4. The person you paid to provide the care was not your spouse or a person you could claim as a dependent. If the person you paid to provide the care was your child, he or she must have been 19 or over by the end of 1985.
5. If you were married at the end of 1985, generally, you must file a joint tax return. However, there are two exceptions to this rule. You will be treated as unmarried and still be eligible to take the credit if:

   a. You were legally separated; or

   b. You were living apart from your spouse during the last 6 months of the year, and:

      The qualifying person lived with you in your home over 6 months, and

      You provided over half the cost of keeping up your home.

If your spouse was a full-time student or was mentally or physically unable to care for himself or herself, figure your spouse's earned income on a monthly basis to determine your spouse's earned income for the year. For each month that your spouse was disabled or a full-time student, your spouse is considered to have earned income of not less than $200 a month ($400 a month if more than one qualifying person was cared for in 1985).

If, in the same month, both you and your spouse were full-time students and did not work, you may not use any amount paid that month to figure the credit. The same applies to a couple who did not work because neither was capable of self-care.

The amount of the child care credit is 30 percent of work related expenses if your adjusted gross income is $10,000 or less. The 30 percent is reduced by one percent for each $2,000 of your adjusted gross income, or part of $2,000, above $10,000 until the percentage is reduced to 20 percent for income above $28,000. A chart for the applicable percentage is provided on Form 2441, Credit for Child Care and Dependent Care Expenses.

The most child care credit you can take to reduce your tax in any year is $720 if your expenses are for one qualifying individual or $1,440 if expenses are for two or more.

The credit is available to married couples if one works full-time and the other part-time or is a full-time student. The amount is limited to the earnings of the spouse with the lower income. If one spouse is a student or is incapable of self-care and so has no earned income, the law presumes an income of $200 per month if there is one dependent and $400 per month for two or more whether there is, in fact, any income at all. If you are considered "married" for federal tax purposes, you must file a joint return with your husband to qualify for this credit.

WHAT KINDS OF INCOME MIGHT BE SIGNIFICANT TO ME AS A WOMAN TAXPAYER?

If you are receiving temporary or permanent alimony, you have to pay tax on it if you are above the zero bracket amount.[25] Under some circumstances, you may also have to pay capital gains tax, when you transfer appreciated property in a divorced property settlement if the transfer was prior to 19 July 1984.[26]

Generally, the gain or loss is the difference between the adjusted basis of the property and its fair market value at the time of the transfer. If the property has increased in value, there may be a taxable gain; a decrease in value would result in a loss. However, a loss is only deductible if the property is business or investment property.

The spouse making the transfer would realize the gain or loss on the transfer. An equal division of co-owned property does not result in a gain or a loss. See IRS publication 504, "Tax Information for Divorced or Separated Individuals," for additional information.

Support for a minor child is not taxed as income to you; however, unless the divorce decree or separation agreement specifies an amount of child support, the entire payment you receive will be considered alimony.[27]

Under recent Utah law changes, Utah Code 78-45d-l, et. seq. effective 1 July 1985, the state may withhold delinquent support payments from the paychecks of the noncustodial parent. The law allows for the custodial parent to have such an order included in his or her divorce papers or to obtain such an order after child support payments become delinquent. For further information, call the State Division of Recovery Services.

If you have an adopted child, payments you receive from a state agency to help you care for the child are not subject to income tax,[28] but you can't count that money as child support you furnished in claiming a dependency exemption for that child.

Awards in a Title VII suit are also considered taxable "wages." (See Chapter 7, "Employment.") Unemployment benefits from a private program are taxable to the extent the amounts you receive exceed the amounts you contributed to the program.[29] For example, government-sponsored unemployment compensation, as of 1979, is taxed after your total annual income exceeds the certain "base amount exemption" discussed earlier.[30] Amounts withheld from your paycheck for union dues or other union payments are part of your taxable income.

Social security benefits, including OASDI (Old Age Survivor Disability Insurance) benefits, are not taxable income.[31] Generally, most forms of public assistance or general welfare payments are not subject to income tax. However, some higher income retirees who receive Social Security benefits will have to pay federal income tax on part of their benefits, including single Social Security recipients whose 1984 taxable income, including Social Security income, is expected to be more than $25,000, and married Social Security recipients whose 1984 joint income will exceed $32,000. To have adequate tax withheld, these individuals may need to file and pay quarterly estimated taxes on Form 1040-ES, Estimated Tax for Individuals.

For more information on the new tax on some Social Security benefits and on estimated taxes, see Publication 505, "Tax Withholding and Estimated Tax."

Babysitting income, tips and gratuities, are also taxable income.

If you are a widow, proceeds of a life insurance policy on your husband's life are not taxable income.[32] Certain death benefits that your deceased husband's employer may pay you are taxed only to the extent that the payment exceeds $5,000.[33] If you are the executor of your husband's estate, your fees, if any, are taxable income.

If you or your husband serve in the military, Family Separation Allowances received because of overseas assignments are excluded from your taxable income.[34] If you are the widow of a serviceman who died in active service, death gratuity benefits you receive from the government are not taxable,[35] nor are benefits you receive from the Serviceman's Group Life Insurance program.[36]

WHERE CAN I GET MORE INFORMATION ON FEDERAL INCOME TAXES?

Federal income tax forms contain detailed instructions. The IRS also publishes a series of free pamphlets, the Taxpayer Information Series, available at your local IRS office. Call your local IRS office or call the toll-free number listed in your telephone directory.

WHAT ABOUT UTAH INCOME TAX LAWS?

Utah income tax laws are similar to the federal income tax code. In Utah, married taxpayers may file jointly or separately; but if you filed separate federal income tax returns, you must file separate returns in Utah. If you filed a joint federal return, you can choose to file separate Utah returns, dividing up nonbusiness deductions as you like. This includes deciding who gets some of the personal exemptions, like those for a dependent child or relative.

The number of personal exemptions allowable are the same as those permitted under federal tax law. The amount excluded from income per exemptions is $750.

The state of Utah follows the Federal Income Tax Forms 1040 and 1040A by taking most figures directly off your Federal Income Tax Return and adjusting entries where appropriate.

WHEN MUST I PAY TAXES ON GIFTS?

You do not pay gift taxes when you get a gift, but you are liable for federal gift taxes whenever you make a gift or transfer property without getting anything of adequate value in return. In Utah, gift tax functions in much the same way as the federal gift tax.

IS EVERY GIFT SUBJECT TO FILING A FORM 709, UNITED STATES GIFT TAX RETURN?

Generally, the Federal Gift Tax applies to any gift of real or personal property, whether tangible or intangible, that you give directly, in trust, or by any other means to a donee.

Under federal law you may, without paying tax, give $10,000[37] per year per person to as many individuals as you wish. If you are married, you and your husband may together give up to $20,000 per year per person.[38]

Under the federal gift-tax marital deduction, you may give any gift to your spouse without incurring a gift tax liability. Many couples with this kind of income use the marital gift provision to reduce the amount of the estate—which is taxed heavily when someone dies. Federal estate and gift tax law also allows you a "Unified Credit"[39] of $121,800 in 1985, $155,800 in 1986 and $192,800 thereafter. In effect, this credit allows you to transfer $400,000 in 1985, $500,000 in 1986 and $600,000 thereafter.

Gifts to charities are tax-exempt under state gift tax law and deductible under federal gift tax law.[40]

WHAT IS AN ESTATE TAX?

When you die and your property—any property in which you had an interest—goes to others, the IRS taxes the transfer. The amount of tax is determined by the size of the estate (the amount of property you owned or had an interest in) and is payable out of the estate. Estate tax rates[41] are high, when fully implemented, from 37 percent on the first dollar over $400,000 in 1985 on taxable transfers to a high of 50 percent on taxable transfers over $2.5 million.

Utah does not have an inheritance tax—a tax you pay on property received when someone dies. Utah tax is paid from the estate when federal estate taxes are due. This tax is maximum credit for state death taxes computed for federal estate tax purposes[42] i.e., the date of death in 1990 of a single taxpayer with a $750,000 taxable estate. The Federal Tax *before unified credit* is $248,300. As of 1987, Unified Credit would cover $192,800 of that tax liability; therefore, the estate would only be required to pay the difference between $192,800 and $248,300, or $55,500.

ARE ALL ESTATES SUBJECT TO THE FEDERAL ESTATE TAX?

Because of the unified estate and gift tax credit mentioned above, only estates under the Unified Credit are exempt from this tax. As of 1987, the unified Credit of $192,800 exempts the first $600,000 of estate and taxable gift assets. If your assets are greater than the Unified Credit exempt amount, you may pass more than this amount tax-free at your death if you are eligible for a marital deduction. (See the next two questions.) In any event, if you believe that you and your husband have combined assets exceeding the Unified Credit exempt amount or that your own estate will be greater than the Unified Credit exempt amount upon your death, you should talk to an estate planner.

HOW CAN I OR MY HUSBAND USE THE FEDERAL ESTATE TAX MARITAL DEDUCTION?

Under federal estate tax law, you may take advantage of the marital deduction[43] if you leave property to your surviving spouse at your death. The marital deduction lets you reduce your otherwise taxable estate by the value of property left to your surviving spouse.

This deduction is available in addition to the unified credit; thus with careful planning, either you or your husband could conceivably leave an estate which would go untaxed. Saving taxes this way can be crucial to the preservation of a family farm or business.

SHOULD YOU ALWAYS USE A FULL MARITAL DEDUCTION?

Although we have an unlimited marital deduction it is not always advantageous to use the maximum marital deduction allowed to you as a surviving spouse. For example, a married couple has $1,000,000 estate and the Unified Credit exempts the first $500,000. If the surviving spouse took the full $1,000,000 marital deduction the taxable estate would be zero. However, when the surviving spouse dies the estate will pay $92,500 in estate taxes.

But if, in the same example, the surviving spouse received only $500,000 as a marital deduction (with the other $500,000 going to the children or other individuals) there would be a taxable estate of $500,000. Because the Unified Credit exempts the first $500,000, there would be no tax. When the surviving spouse dies, his or her estate would also be $500,000 (assuming no acquisition or appreciation). With the $500,000 exempted by the Unified Credit, there would again be no estate tax.

WHAT UTAH PROPERTY TAXES MUST I PAY ?

Both real and personal property in Utah are taxed by the county you live in. You pay the county assessor, for instance, taxes on your car (personal) and your house (real) every year.

6 Social Welfare Laws

WHAT ARE UTAH'S BASIC SOCIAL WELFARE PROGRAMS?

The federal Social Security Act of 1935 established several programs designed to guarantee a minimum level of economic benefits for everyone. Today these programs include Social Security, a system of basic income security for most retired and disabled workers and their dependents, and for survivors of deceased workers (RSHDI); hospital and medical insurance for the aged and disabled (Medicare); health care and services for low income persons (Medicaid); benefits for those—usually coal miners—suffering from black lung; supplemental security income for people sixty-five or older, blind, or disabled (SSI); unemployment insurance, and general public assistance and welfare services.

While these programs are designed for all citizens, certain aspects may be particularly relevant to working women, working wives or mothers, and homemakers.

The actual dollar amounts and other requirements may change from year to year, but you could contact one of these agencies to determine the current status of a provision: Utah Legal Services (328-8891), Utahns Against Hunger (328-2561), or Utah Issues (521-2035).

WHAT ABOUT SOCIAL SECURITY (RSHDI)?

Retirement, Survivors, Disability, and Health Insurance (RSHDI) is a federally funded retirement insurance program for American workers.[1] Commonly called "Social Security," it is a government-administered insurance fund which employees pay into during their working years and from which they collect benefits when they either retire or become disabled. It provides monthly cash benefits as a substitute for earned income to workers who are retired or totally disabled, to their dependents, and, after they die, to their surviving dependents.

Because the amount of monthly benefits you will receive is based on your average earnings, you should be sure each of your employers has your correct Social Security number and accurately reports your wages and the amount being withheld to the Social Security Administration. Before you are entitled to monthly benefits you must work for a certain amount of time, which is figured in three-month periods or quarters. The amount of work time necessary for monthly benefits depends on the year in which you reach age sixty-two or the date of your death or disability or your spouse's death or disability.[2] Generally, a worker with fewer than six quarters (that is, one and one-half years or eighteen months) of employment will not qualify for regular old-age benefits. No one needs more than ten years of work to be eligible for benefits.

IF I WORK OUTSIDE MY HOME, WILL MY FAMILY AND I RECEIVE SOCIAL SECURITY BENEFITS?

As a working woman, you earn Social Security protection not only for yourself but also for your dependents. Even if you have no dependents, the Social Security credit you earn while you work counts toward monthly benefits for the family you may have in the future.

WHEN CAN I RETIRE AND RECEIVE BENEFITS?

If you have worked the necessary number of quarters, you can retire as early as age sixty-two, but you will have to take reduced benefits. Payments to people who retire before age sixty-five are permanently reduced to balance the longer period of time they will receive checks. The reduction formula—5/9 of 1 percent reduction for each month between the sixty-second and sixty-fifth birthdays—is applied against the worker's benefits.[3] This means that if you retire at sixty-two, your monthly benefits would be 20 percent less than the monthly amount you would receive if you retire at sixty-five and you have worked the necessary number of quarters. Similarly, if you retire after age sixty-five, the amount you receive will increase by 3 percent per year.[4]

IF I AM MARRIED, AM I ENTITLED TO MY HUSBAND'S BENEFITS IN ADDITION TO THOSE EARNED FROM MY OWN WORK RECORD?

No. If you are married, you can get retirement payments *either* on your own record *or* on your husband's, whichever will pay the larger benefits.[5] If you have worked all your adult life and have high earnings, it is likely that your own benefits will be higher than those you could receive from your husband's work record. At sixty-five, a wife gets 50 percent of what her husband is entitled to at sixty-five or reduced benefits if she retires at sixty-two. But if you stopped working for several years or had lower earnings, your husband's payment may be higher. When you apply for retirement benefits, the Social Security office should tell you whether your own record or your husband's will pay a higher amount.

In the same way, your husband can get retirement benefits on your record once he is sixty-two if he does not have a record which will pay him more.

WHAT HAPPENS IF I'M DISABLED?

If you become disabled and cannot work for a year or more, you can receive disability benefits.[6] "Disability" is a medical question which must be decided by at least one doctor. There is a Social Security Review Board which scrutinizes medical findings on disability, and it can accept or reject a doctor's recommendation. Disability standards are hard to meet, and the current trend is to make them even stricter. HHS (Health and Human Services), which oversees this program, has established a set of regulations which define "disability." These regulations categorize workers according to age, education, and work experience, and then make certain assumptions.[7] For example, a worker who is fifty-five and over will be presumed "disabled" if she or he has less than a high school education, has worked in only semi-skilled jobs, and has an impairment so severe that she or he can do only sedentary work (work sitting down). If the same worker is between eighteen and forty-four, however, he or she is considered to be "retrainable" and not disabled.

There is a five-month waiting period before you begin receiving disability benefits. Payments begin with the sixth full month of your disability and continue until you reach retirement age and begin to receive retirement benefits. If you have been eligible for disability payments for two consecutive years, you will also have Medicare coverage. If you are disabled, your children (including your stepchildren or legally adopted children) can also receive benefits based on your disability. Monthly benefits based on your disability are payable to your unmarried children under eighteen and to any of your children who become disabled themselves before age twenty-two and remain disabled. If you are getting disability benefits, your husband also qualifies for payment if he is sixty-two or older.

If the Review Board says you are disabled, you may be referred to vocational rehabilitation service counselors who should evaluate your ability to work, provide job training, and help you in job placement. As soon as you can work, you are no longer eligible for disability benefits.

WILL MY FAMILY RECEIVE SOCIAL SECURITY BENEFITS IF I DIE?

Both your spouse and your children can get monthly survivors' benefits if you die. Your family may be entitled to survivors' benefits even if you have only one and one-half years of work in the three years before you die. There is a lump-sum death payment of $255 to help pay funeral expenses. To be eligible for this payment you must be either a surviving spouse who was living with the deceased at the time of their death or separated only due to illness, or a dependent child. If your husband has no young children in his care at your death, he must be sixty or older, or between fifty and sixty and disabled, to qualify for survivors' benefits on your work record. Your spouse will be entitled to benefits regardless of his age, if you are insured, if he has not remarried, and if he has in his care an unmarried child under eighteen or an older child who was disabled before the age of twenty-two.[8]

WHAT IF I INTERRUPT MY CAREER?

You need credit for a minimum amount of work to qualify for any Social Security benefits. If you stop working before you earn enough quarters of coverage, no benefits will be payable.[9] However, credits you earn will remain on your work record, and you can go back to work and earn the additional credits you need to qualify. This rule is particularly significant to you as a woman, since you may prefer to interrupt your career to stay home and raise children.

You should realize, however, that the *amount* of your monthly payments will be affected because you earned no income during the years you chose to remain at home. Your benefits may be somewhat lower since the amount of your payment is based on your average earnings over a period of years.[10] The years in which you had no or low income will lower the average. And, an interruption in your work history *may* make you ineligible for disability benefits. To qualify for disability benefits, you must have worked one-half of the time during the ten years before the disability occurred.[11]

AM I ELIGIBLE FOR SOCIAL SECURITY IF I WORK IN MY HOME?

In most jobs, Social Security contributions are taken from your pay automatically. But this may not be the case if you are a household worker, which includes babysitters, maids, cooks, laundry workers, butlers, gardeners, chauffeurs, and people who do house cleaning or repair work—anyone employed in or around someone else's home.

If you are a household worker and your employer reports your earnings to Social Security, you can get one quarter of Social Security coverage for every $260 you earn. You should, therefore, show your employer your Social Security card and tell her or him to deduct Social Security contributions from your wages. If you don't, you won't get Social Security credit for your work; and if you don't have enough credits, you and your family won't be entitled to monthly benefits based on your work record. However, you may still be entitled to the other types of benefits and assistance discussed in the rest of this chapter.

WHAT IF I EMPLOY A HOUSEHOLD WORKER?

If you employ a household worker, it is your responsibility to see that wages you pay are properly reported. You must deduct Social Security contributions from the wages, pay an equal amount as the employer, and send them to the Internal Revenue Service with a report of total wages paid. The report form and instructions are available at any IRS office.

WHAT IF I CHANGE MY NAME?

You should be sure that your Social Security record shows your correct name, particularly if you are employed, because your employer reports your earnings under the name you give her or him.

Whenever you change the name you use in employment, whether because of marriage, divorce, or other reasons, you should report the change to Social Security.[12] If you choose to continue using your maiden name after marriage you do not have to report your marriage. Just be certain you use your maiden name consistently throughout your employment.

Even if you do not work, you should report any name change so that your record will show the correct name when you apply for benefits. To report a name change, simply fill out a "Request for Change in Social Security Records." You can get this form at any Social Security office.

IF I'VE NEVER BEEN EMPLOYED CAN I RECEIVE BENEFITS BASED ON MY HUSBAND'S RECORD?

If you are a married woman and have never been employed, you are entitled to benefits based on your husband's work record when he becomes disabled or retires if you are caring for a child under eighteen or a disabled child who is entitled to benefits, regardless of your age, or if you do not have a child in your care but are sixty-two or older.[13] You are entitled to full wife's retirement benefits, or 50 percent of the amount your husband is entitled to, if you wait until sixty-five to collect these benefits.[14] If you get benefits before age sixty-five, the payment is permanently reduced.

If you are a widow who has never been employed, you can receive monthly survivors' benefits and your children may also be entitled to survivors' benefits. You can get a widow's benefit at any age if you are caring for a child who is under eighteen or disabled and entitled to benefits. These benefits will stop when you no longer have in your care a child who is under eighteen or disabled. If you are sixty or older when your husband dies, you are entitled to widow's benefits, even if you have no dependent children. If you are fifty and disabled, you are also eligible for these benefits.[15] If you are sixty-five or older at the time of your husband's death, you will get the full amount of payments your husband would have received if he had lived.

If you are collecting benefits on behalf of your deceased husband and you remarry, and if you are *under* sixty, your payments based on his record will stop. You may become re-entitled to these payments if your subsequent marriage ends.[16] If you are *over* sixty, your payments could continue; but if your new husband gets Social Security checks, you can take a wife's benefit on his record if it would be larger than your widow's payment.

IF I GET DIVORCED, WILL I BE ENTITLED TO BENEFITS BASED ON MY EX-HUSBAND'S EARNINGS?

You are entitled to benefits when your ex-husband starts collecting retirement or disability payments if you are sixty-two or older and were married to him for at least ten years.

You may also get payments if your ex-husband dies, provided you are sixty or older (fifty, if you are disabled) and you either were married at least ten years or have young children entitled to benefits on his record.

DOES SOCIAL SECURITY DISCRIMINATE AGAINST ME AS A WOMAN?

Social Security legislation has increasingly been attacked for discriminating on the basis of sex. Although this discrimination results in inequities which can affect both men and women, the inequities in fact fall primarily on women. This is largely because Social Security legislation was enacted at a time when women were assumed to be financially dependent on their husbands and marriage was assumed to be a life-time arrangement. Today, half of all marriages break up and half of all married women work, yet Social Security legislation remains substantially the same as when it was enacted forty years ago.

An example of discrimination against women under present laws is the fact that a person can claim benefits both as a wage earner and as a dependent, yet Social Security is structured so a person, either a man or a woman, cannot get both a full benefit as a wage earner and a full benefit as a non-earning dependent. This may result in a two-income family paying more Social Security taxes on their combined wages, yet receiving fewer overall benefits than a couple with only one wage earner but the same income. Unless a wage-earning wife is entitled to more than half of her husband's primary benefit amount in her own right, she will not receive any additional benefits as a result of her own Social Security earnings and contribution. Although more women are active in the labor force, large numbers of women do not receive significant benefits from their contributions.

Further discrimination against women as a consequence of Social Security law comes from the current practice of averaging earnings to determine benefit amounts. Social Security benefits are based on the worker's average earnings in a specified number of years. Because of this, inflation and typical salary increases throughout a career can combine to create a situation in which the average salary is significantly smaller than the pre-retirement salary. Although this problem exists for both men and women, the consequences for women are much greater, partly because of employment discrimination. In addition, women often spend a period of time bearing and raising children, when they may earn very little or nothing. Women who work part-time or part of a year will have low annual earnings. A pattern of absences from the labor force seriously affects the woman's right to disability benefits. Since the law does not currently view housework and homemaking as a valid occupation, a woman who spends years of her life in such labor may end up with little or no security in her old age. And, under current legislation, when a marriage lasts less than ten years, a divorced homemaker receives *no* Social Security benefits.

This discrimination has been considered by the Department of Health, Education, and Welfare. The Department has offered two proposals. One is a "shared earnings" approach, where family earnings would be pooled and each partner would be credited with half the total in computing benefits. The other is a "two-tier" approach, where a basic monthly benefit of $122 would be provided to each spouse over sixty-five, with an additional sum based on individual earnings. Either approach would ease many of the inequities found in the current system.

WHERE CAN I GET MORE INFORMATION?

If you would like to learn more or get a statement of your contributions to date, you can write to:

Social Security Administration
6401 Security Boulevard
Baltimore, Maryland 21235

Include your Social Security number and birthdate as identification. If you want to apply for benefits or need additional information, you can call your local Social Security office, which is listed under Social Security Administration in your local telephone book.

WHAT IS SUPPLEMENTAL SECURITY INCOME (SSI)?

SSI is a federal cash benefit program that pays monthly benefits to people in financial need who are sixty-five or older and to blind or disabled people of any age who are in need.[17]

The aim of the program is to provide a basic cash income to people who have no income or a very small one. The amount of SSI payments you receive depends on your income and the value of any assets such as property you may own. Income you receive from Social Security, veteran's compensation, pensions, and gifts generally reduces the amount of your SSI payment.[18]

In 1985, the amount an individual can receive each month is $325.30. A couple can receive up to $488.00. When you apply for SSI benefits, the amount of income you receive from other sources is computed; and if it is below these levels, you will receive an additional check each month from SSI to bring your income up to the SSI benefit level. There is also a state supplement of $10. However, a slight reduction in the state supplement is scheduled to begin in January of 1987.

To be eligible for SSI you must be in financial need and be over sixty-five; or blind (vision no better than 20/200 even with glasses, or 'tunnel vision', or limited visual field of 20 degrees or less); or "disabled," which means you cannot engage in substantial gainful work because of a physical or mental impairment which has, or is expected to, last twelve months or which can be expected to result in death.

SSI recipients are almost always eligible for food stamps and Medicaid, but you must apply for them separately. Because SSI is administered by the Social Security Administration, you should contact that agency to apply or to ask questions.

WHAT IS MEDICARE?

Contributions made to Social Security also fund Medicare. Medicare eligibility is based on your Social Security coverage and work history; you do not have to be in a low-income bracket to receive Medicare. You are eligible for Medicare if you are sixty-five and are eligible for Social Security or railroad retirement benefits either as a retired worker or as the spouse or widow of a retired worker; or if you are disabled and have been receiving disability benefits for twenty-four months; or if you have end stage renal disease and have required dialysis or kidney transplant.[19]

Medicare has two parts: Part A, or hospital insurance, covers the cost of hospitalization, "extended care" provided by a hospital when you are not hospitalized, and home health care agencies. You automatically get hospital insurance if you qualify for Social Security benefits. If you don't have enough quarters of coverage to qualify, you can purchase the insurance for a yearly premium that changes each year. (It cost $174 a year in 1985.)

Part B, medical insurance, covers medical and other health services, including a doctor's care. Unless you buy Part A, hospital insurance, the medical insurance is optional and the price varies from year to year. (It cost $15.50 a month in 1985.) The amount will be deducted from your Social Security check. You can sign up for Part B only during a "general enrollment period," each year from January 1 to March 31. There is a penalty of 10 percent of the premium for each year over sixty-five if you have delayed enrollment.

It is a good idea to apply for your Medicare insurance three months before the month in which you turn sixty-five. That means your coverage will begin the month of your birthday. Otherwise, there may be some delay. You can also apply during the three months after your sixty-fifth birthday. When you apply for Part A, hospital insurance, you will be automatically enrolled for Part B, medical insurance, unless you tell the Social Security office you do not want it.

For more information on Medicare and the exact services Parts A and B cover, call or write your local Social Security office. The telephone number is listed under the Social Security Administration in your local telephone book.

WHAT IS MEDICAID?

Medicaid is a federal- and state-funded program run by the state, which provides medical insurance for people with low incomes.[20] Eligible persons receive a card which they can present to doctors, druggists, hospitals, and other health care providers. Bills for medical services to card holders are sent to the state for payment, following a specific schedule of fees.

You are eligible for Medicaid if you receive SSI (see earlier section) or AFDC (see following section), but you must make separate application for it. You may also qualify if you are "medically needy," a term that means your income and resources are insufficient, in comparison with a standard set by the state, to pay for your medical care. If you are medically needy, you are responsible for your medical bills equal to the amount your income is above the Medicaid eligibility point. Medicaid will pay the rest of your medical bills. In Utah, many elderly people as well as low-income families qualify for Medicaid through a medically needy status.

Medicaid now provides many services in Utah, but because each state can limit the type of service provided, there are frequent changes in Medicaid services. Currently covered Medicaid services include hospital care, out-patient service like X-rays and laboratory services, doctor's fees, nursing home care, transportation for medical services (which must be authorized in advance except in emergencies), prescription drugs, some dental services, eye examinations and glasses, and sterilizations and abortions in limited circumstances.

WHAT IS AID TO FAMILIES WITH DEPENDENT CHILDREN (AFDC)?

AFDC is federally funded financial aid. The program, which is operated by the state, is intended to benefit needy, dependent children who have lost parental care and support because of the death, severe mental or physical problems, or the continued absence from home of one or both parents. If you are a parent or relative providing parental care and guidance (including a home for a needy child), you may apply for AFDC at your local Community Operations office, listed under State Social Services. Someone in that office will explain your rights, responsibilities, eligibility requirements, and methods of deciding how much money your family may receive if it is eligible.

Financial need is the key factor in deciding if your family will receive aid. Need is determined by the Community Operations office. To be eligible for AFDC, you must meet certain conditions.[21] The child must be a resident of Utah, a citizen of the United States, and, if under eighteen, regularly attending school; the child must also be deprived of "parental support or care by reason of death, continued absence from the home, or physical or mental incapacity of a parent" and the child must be living with one of her/his parents or a "specified relative" (brother, sister, uncle, aunt, nephew, niece, grandparent, step-parent, or relative by adoption or marriage).

The child must also be in financial need, which means that the total "countable" income for the household where the child is living is less than the standard set for the state. In addition, the total resources of the household must be within the state-determined limit of $1,000 excluding household property unless any item is valued at $1,000 or more. The standard of financial need and the amount you may receive varies with the amount of "countable" income and the number of people in the household. There are limits on the amount that can be paid. The amount payable is currently 53 percent of the standard needs budget, or the amount established by the state as necessary to meet the basic needs of a household.[22] Consequently, most AFDC households also apply for food stamps and Medicaid. Each adult family member asking for or receiving help under this program must register for work at Job Service except for those who are ill or incapacitated, sixty-five or older, required in the home to care for another member of the family who is ill, or responsible for the care of a child under six. However, as the parent or guardian you have the right to volunteer for the work and training program and a right to child care services so you can participate in this program. Apply for AFDC in the state welfare office of the city or county where the child lives.

WHAT ARE FOOD STAMPS?

Until 1 January 1979, participants in the food stamp program paid a certain amount of money ("purchase price") based on family size, income, and expenses. In return, they received food stamp coupons worth more than the purchase price ("bonus amount"). After 1 January 1979, the purchase price was eliminated, and families were given only the bonus amount. This meant that instead of paying $100 for $150 in food stamps, the family now keeps the $100 in cash and receives only the $50 bonus in food stamps.

The local state welfare office has the responsibility of deciding who receives food stamps and what the benefits are for each person.

HOW DO I KNOW IF I AM ELIGIBLE FOR FOOD STAMPS?

The Food Stamp Act of 1977 changed the food stamp program dramatically. Part of this act eliminated the purchase price requirement described above. Other provisions of the act, designed to make food stamps easier to get, went into effect 1 March 1979.

Food stamps are given to "households," that is groups of people who usually buy, store, and prepare their food together. Single people can constitute a one-person household. Households do not include roomers or boarders. You qualify for food stamps if your income, minus certain deductions, falls below a certain level and your resources are below a set limit. The maximum amount of food stamps a four-person household may receive is $264 a month. The resource limit of most households is $1,500. If you have two or more in your household, and one is over sixty, the resource limit is $3,000. "Resources" are land, goods, money or stocks which can be sold. Your house and all adjoining land, your household furnishings, your car (up to $4,500 in value) and other items are *not* counted as resources.[23]

HOW DO I APPLY FOR FOOD STAMPS?

You apply for food stamps by going to your local state Community Operations office. You have a right to fill out and submit an application on the same day you go in. If you do not have all the information you need at that time, you may submit an application anyway.

You have a right to do this on the same day you go in, because the welfare office has only thirty days from the time you submit the application to either get food stamps to you or to tell you your application has been denied.

WHAT IF I NEED FOOD STAMPS IN A HURRY?

Under certain circumstances, a household may be eligible for fast or "expedited service."[24] If the family has less than $100 in cash, and has a household income of less than $150 per month, or if the family is that of migrant or seasonal farm workers, or if the household simply has no income, it is eligible. A battered woman in shelter placement may be entitled to a second allotment of food stamps if she received the first while she was still in the household with the abusive spouse.

If you qualify for expedited service, many of the normal application procedures are postponed. You only need to prove your identity through a driver's license, work or school I.D., SSA verification, voter registration card, etc. Your rent receipt is adequate to prove your address. Once you have done this, you will be able to have your food stamps *by the fifth calendar day* after you apply.

Contact your local Community Operations office for further information about food stamps. This office should be listed under Social Services Department with the other state offices.

IF I AM OUT OF WORK, CAN I COLLECT UNEMPLOYMENT COMPENSATION?

The unemployment insurance program provides temporary financial help to workers who meet certain requirements and who are out of work through no "fault" of their own.[25] "Fault" is a legal term which is frequently argued. Basically it means that you weren't fired or that you didn't quit without "good cause." Sexual harassment on the job is recognized in Utah as "good cause," and a woman who quits her job because of such harassment is entitled to unemployment.

The Utah Department of Employment Security commonly known as Job Service, manages the program, and all claims or inquiries should be filed through that office. There are local offices in most counties.

Unemployment insurance payments are paid by employer and employee contributions.

You are eligible for such payments if you have been working at a job and federal payroll tax has been deducted from your pay check for at least twenty-six weeks. If you are eligible, the size of your payments and how long you can receive them depends on how long you worked and how much you earned.[26] Basically, to be eligible in Utah, you must fulfill the prior earnings requirement, have twenty-six weeks of deductions, and not be unemployed because of a labor dispute in which you, or a class of workers you belong to, have participated, financed, or taken a direct interest. You must not be receiving other unemployment compensation or be on a bona fide vacation. You must also register to work at the local Job Service office when you file your claim and continue to report there at least once a week. You must be able to work and be available to work. That means you must look for a job and not impose unreasonable conditions on a future job.

WILL I GET UNEMPLOYMENT BENEFITS IF I STOP WORKING BECAUSE I AM PREGNANT?

Although there are no specific provisions in the Utah Employment Compensation Law about pregnancy, it is possible that pregnant women will face additional problems in meeting eligibility requirements.

The law requires that a person asking for these benefits be "able" to work. Your pregnancy will eventually interfere with your ability to work, at least for some period of time. Recently the United States Supreme Court ruled that an individual's ability to work had to be determined on a case-by-case basis, and that the state could not expect inability to work simply because of a pregnancy.[27]

If you decide to leave your job because you are pregnant, but you are still physically able to work, you may be entitled to unemployment if you can prove that you are, in fact, still able to work. The fact that you have left your job on your own will also be considered, but that does not automatically mean you are ineligible. If you have taken maternity leave because you are no longer physically able to work, you cannot receive unemployment benefits since everyone receiving unemployment must be currently able to work and available for work. If you have any problems as a pregnant woman seeking unemployment benefits, you should contact an attorney or a legal aid society.

WILL I BE PAID WORKER'S COMPENSATION IF I AM INJURED ON THE JOB?

If you are injured because of an accident that happened while you were actually working, or you are suffering from an "occupational disease" caused by the type of work you perform, you can receive money under the Utah Worker's Compensaton Act.[28]

If you believe you have such an injury or disease, you should give your employer written notice as soon as possible, within at least forty-eight hours of the injury. You must also file a claim with the state Industrial Commission within three years of the accident, or the week in which you last received compensation payments, to be eligible for compensation. For more information, contact:

The Industrial Commission of Utah
Department of Employment Security
Claims Department
Heber M. Wells Building
Salt Lake City, Utah 84111
Telephone: (801) 533-6411

WHAT CAN I DO IF I THINK I AM BEING TREATED UNFAIRLY BY ANY OF THESE AGENCIES?

It is always possible that an agency office has made a mistake about a claim you have made. If you feel the agency has discriminated against you, did not process your claim correctly, improperly stopped your benefits, or failed to give you the benefits you legally deserve, you should insist on an explanation. If you still do not agree with the decision of the agency, you should immediately contact an attorney or Utah Legal Services, file a written complaint with your local office, and request a fair hearing. At the hearing stage, it is especially important that you have an attorney.

7 Employment

WHAT IS THE CURRENT ECONOMIC SITUATION OF WORKING WOMEN?

According to the "Governor's Report on Utah Women in Economic Crisis," June 1984, there is a growing crisis for women in the state of Utah. In 1980, 23,125 families were headed by women, single heads of household in Utah. Fifty percent of the families headed by women, single heads of households were in poverty. In 1979 there were 56,986 children in poverty. In other words, the statistical probability of being poor is tied directly to being a woman. The way to combat the economic crisis faced by women is through meaningful employment which will enable women to support themselves and their families.

Furthermore, on the average a working woman makes 63 cents for every dollar a man makes. One of the barriers to meaningful employment is discrimination, or treating men workers and women workers differently on the basis of gender.

There is a growing awareness that women are a legitimate component in today's workforce. Economic demands and personal goals lead many women to consider careers, rather than merely jobs. One barrier to full employment of women will be removed when discrimination is completely eliminated.

Many laws and executive orders prohibit discrimination in employment. The laws governing an employee's rights to nondiscriminatory treatment are complicated and confusing. Each of the major federal laws is different from the others, varying in the range of employers covered, the types of discrimination prohibited, the scope of protection provided, and the methods of enforcement by federal agencies or by individuals.

You should always assert your rights under as many of the laws as possible. The procedures under each law are separate and independent from each other. Since you must comply with each law's procedures and time limits, it is sometimes wise to consult a lawyer for help with employment discrimination claims.

WHAT FEDERAL LAWS ADDRESS DISCRIMINATION IN EMPLOYMENT?

There are two ways the federal government creates laws about discrimination in employment. Congress can pass legislation and the President of the United States can issue executive orders. Here are some of the most important laws that you, as a woman, should know about regarding your employment.

1. *Title VII of the Civil Rights Act of 1964* is by far the most comprehensive and most widely used employment discrimination law. It is also the most specific, prohibiting virtually all forms of discrimination. It forbids practices which are intentionally discriminatory as well as those which have a discriminatory effect.

Title VII was inacted to prohibit employment discrimination on the basis of race, color, religion, sex, or national origin by private employers. It has since been amended (1972) to prohibit the same sorts of discrimination by state, local, or federal government units.

Title VII created the Equal Employment Opportunity Commission (EEOC) which administers and enforces the act. A complaint under Title VII must be filed with the EEOC or a state human rights agency before it can be taken to court. Title VII will be discussed in greater detail later in this chapter.

2. *The Equal Pay Act of 1963* (EPA) says that equal pay must be given for substantially equal work performed by women and men in the same company or government office.

"Equal work" means tasks requiring equal skill, effort, responsibility, and/or training. The tasks should be substantially similar but need not be identical. For example, the pay of a female bookkeeper can be compared to that of a male bookkeeper working on a different ledger, but not to that of a male clerk.

This law does not apply to pay differences unrelated to sex. For example, it is legal to pay more according to seniority, merit, or other systems that reward worker productivity.

The EPA covers most private employees and federal, state, and local government employees, including executive, administrative, and professional employees. Technically, companies covered by this law are those "engaged in commerce." It has been interpreted broadly to cover nearly all employers.

The EPA is administered by the EEOC, but unlike a Title VII claim, you may, under the EPA, file a suit directly in court.

3. *The Age Discrimination in Employment Act of 1967* (AEDA) prohibits age discrimination against individuals between the ages of forty and seventy. (If you have a federal job, there is no maximum age.)

The AEDA applies to employers of twenty or more persons, employment agencies, labor unions with more than twenty-five members and public employers. It prohibits discrimination in hiring, firing, training, promotion, compensation, or other terms, conditions, or privileges of employment.

For example, an employer may not discharge an older, more expensive employee to hire a younger worker who will cost the company less in salary and benefits.

However, the ADEA does not prohibit discrimination based on *necessary* job qualifications or standards of performance. Thus, a sixty-five year old employee can be fired if he or she simply *cannot* do the job. But so long as the employee can perform the job, it is illegal to fire the person because of his or her age.

The EEOC administers and enforces the ADEA. Claims under this law should be filed with the EEOC.

4. *The Rehabilitation Act of 1973* prohibits discrimination in employment on the basis of physical or mental handicap.

Handicap means, according to the EEOC, a physical or mental impairment which substantially limits one or more life activities such as caring for one's self, performing manual tasks, walking, seeing, hearing, speaking, breathing, learning, and working.

"Mental impairment" means any psychological disorder or condition, physical impairment, cosmetic disfigurement, or anatomical loss. Included would be mental retardation and other related mental impairment.

Employers must accommodate the handicaps of otherwise qualified individuals.

"Reasonable accommodation" applies to known physical or mental limitations of a qualified handicapped applicant or employee unless those would impose "undue hardship" on its business. "Accommodation" may include, but is not limited to making facilities readily accessible to and usable by handicapped individuals (like restroom stalls large enough for wheelchairs), restructuring jobs to allow part-time or modified work schedules to someone, acquiring or modifying equipment or devices, adjusting or modifying examinations (for instance, reading the questions to a blind applicant), and providing readers for blind people and interpreters for the deaf and other similar actions.

These provisions govern federal agencies, but the Utah Anti-Discrimination Act of 1965, as amended, basically provides identical protection.

Contact the EEOC for information regarding filing claims under this law.

5. *Executive Order 11246,* as amended by Order Number 11375, and Executive Order 11478 prohibit discrimination on the basis of race, color, religion, sex, or national origin in federal offices or in companies which have contracts with the federal government.

Businesses with contracts over $50,000 and fifty or more employees are required to take affirmative action, that is, to establish goals and timetables for full and equal employment opportunities. The Labor Department monitors this law through its Office of Federal Contracts Compliance Program, Federal Building, 125 South State, Salt Lake City, Utah 84147, (801) 524-4470. This office can tell you the dollar amounts per contractor that are needed to qualify.

6. *The Fair Labor Standards Act of 1938* provides for fair labor standards in companies involved in interstate commerce or providing services.

It establishes minimum wage, overtime pay, recordkeeping and child labor standards for full-time and part-time workers and covers federal, state, and local government employees. The only exceptions are schools, hospitals, fire prevention, police protection, public health, and parks and recreation.

Retail and service establishments must gross $362,500 to come under FSLA. Other types of enterprises with a lesser amount of gross volume annual sales are also covered.

Covered employees must be paid for all hours worked in a work week—all time an employee must be on duty or on the employer's premises or at any other prescribed place of work—including additional time that the employee is allowed or permitted to work.

Overtime pay must be at least one and one-half times the employee's regular pay rate for each hour worked.

The wage and Hour Division Department of Labor enforces and administers the act with respect to private employment, state and local government employment, and federal employees of the Library of

Congress, U.S. Postal Service, Postal Rate Commission, and the Tennessee Valley Authority. The Office of Personnel Management is responsible for all other federal employees. The Utah office is Wage-Hour Division, U.S. Department of Labor, Federal Building, 125 South State Street, Salt Lake City, Utah 84147, (801) 524-5706.

If you enter a complaint, FLSA-authorized representatives conduct investigations and gather data about wages, hours, and other employment conditions or practices to determine compliance with the act.

Where violations are found, the investigators may recommend changes in employment practices. Willful violations may be prosecuted criminally and the violator fined up to $10,000. A second conviction may result in imprisonment.

Violators of the child labor provisions are subject to a civil penalty of up to $1,000 for each violation.

It is also a violation to fire or harass an employee for filing a complaint or participating in legal proceedings under the law.

ARE THERE STATE LAWS TO STOP DISCRIMINATION ON THE JOB?

Yes, and like federal laws they have been created two ways: by the state legislature and by executive order of the governor.

1. The *Utah State Fair Employment Practices Act* also called the *Utah Anti-Discrimination Act* was passed in 1965 and amended in 1975. It prohibits discrimination in employment because of race, creed, color, sex, age, religion, ancestry, national origin, handicap, and age if the individual is forty years of age or older.
2. The *Governor's Code of Fair Practices*, Executive Order of May 4, 1979, prohibits discrimination in employment because of race, color, sex, religion, national origin, age, or handicap, for all state agencies and state contractors, including state licensing and regulatory agencies.
3. The Governor's Executive Order of 6 December 1973 created the Office of Equal Employment Opportunity Program and requires state agencies to have Affirmative Action Plans (AAP).

WHAT CAN TITLE VII DO FOR ME?

You will be protected by Title VII if you work or apply for a job with any of the following groups: private employers of fifteen or more employees; federal, state, and local governments; educational institutions, public and private; and labor organizations, including labor-management committees for apprenticeship and training.

Utah law varies only slightly on these matters. The Utah Anti-Discrimination Act prohibits discrimination based on race, religion, color, sex, age, ancestry, national origin, age, and handicap for employees or applicants for jobs where there are twenty-five or more employees. The act excludes religious organizations, associations or corporations, or any other corporation or association that is owned by a religious organization, association or corporation, or a bona fide private membership club (other than a labor organization).

WHAT TYPES OF JOB DISCRIMINATION DOES TITLE VII COVER?

Title VII prohibits discrimination in classified advertisements which list a job preference (for example, "job opportunities—women"). It forbids discriminatory testing for new applicants or for promotions. All testing must be for a true measure of job performance.

Title VII prohibits discriminatory recruitment as well as hiring or firing for discriminatory reasons. For example, an employer cannot fire a woman because she "didn't fit in" with male employees. The act also says compensation, assignment, or classification of employees cannot be discriminatory nor can transfer, promotion, layoff, or recall. An employer cannot pay different salaries because one worker is a male and the other is a female.

Use of company facilities and participation in training and apprenticeship programs must be equally available.

Title VII forbids discrimination in fringe benefits, such as life and health insurance, retirement plans, and disability leave. (The exceptions to these two areas relate to pregnancy and are discussed in the section on pregnancy.) Title VII also protects employees who use the procedures described in EEO legislation. It is unlawful to retaliate against an employee who files a charge of discrimination against a company. The employer cannot harass, demote, terminate, etc., an employee who has filed a charge of discrimination.

DOES TITLE VII COVER EMPLOYMENT AGENCIES?

Yes. It states that it is illegal for employment agencies to discriminate against their own employees on the basis of race, color, religion, sex, or national origin. Agencies cannot discriminate when receiving, classifying, or referring applicants for jobs (for example, referring a woman to a traditional "woman's job" when she is qualified for other work), or when they write classified ads. They are also forbidden to retaliate against anyone—clients or employees—who oppose illegal employment practices or try to use Title VII to stop discrimination.

DOES TITLE VII SAY ANYTHING ABOUT LABOR UNIONS?

Yes. It states that it is illegal for labor unions to discriminate as to who can join, how members are classified, referrals for employment, training and apprenticeship programs, or classified ads. Title VII also says unions cannot discriminate on the basis of sex when they provide fringe benefits like retirement, health, and life insurance plans.

Unions cannot cause an employer to discriminate or retaliate against anyone who opposes illegal employment practices.

WHEN IS "SEX" A LEGAL JOB REQUIREMENT?

Identifying a particular gender for a job is lawful if such requirement is a bona fide occupational qualification (BFOQ), e.g., actor (male, actress female). Saying only men or women can do a certain job must be justified in terms of the particular requirement for the specific job. For example, an employer cannot advertise for "salesmen" only. Anyone with the required experience may apply. Being male is not a BFOQ for selling. Similarly, women cannot be excluded from such jobs as telephone linemen on the basis of the job being dangerous. It is no more dangerous for a woman than it is for a man.

WHAT IS SEXUAL HARASSMENT? DOES IT MEAN THAT PHYSICAL CONTACT WAS MADE OR ATTEMPTED?

Not necessarily. Sexual harassment is defined by the Equal Employment Opportunity Commission (EEOC) as "unwelcome sexual advances, requests for sexual favors, and other *verbal* or *physical conduct* of a sexual nature." You have been sexually harassed if anyone suggested or told you outright that you would have to submit to such conduct or you would not get (or keep) your job.

You've been harassed if submission to or rejection of such conduct was used as a basis for decisions about your job.

If sexual talk or action "unreasonably interferes" with your work performance, or if it creates any intimidating, hostile, or offensive working environment, you have been sexually harassed. You should consult the EEOC or an attorney to determine whether you have any legal recourse.

Not only women are sexually harassed. It is also illegal for women to sexually harass men. For example, a woman supervisor cannot make sexual advances toward a male subordinate.

HOW CAN I TELL WHETHER I AM BEING ASKED DISCRIMINATORY QUESTIONS DURING A JOB INTERVIEW?

The Equal Employment Opportunity Commission regulations do not give a list of questions that are expressly prohibited or improper. In practice, however, EEOC has stated that it looks with "extreme disfavor" on inquiries about race, color, religion, or national origin. The only exceptions are instances where such characteristics are genuine occupational qualifications. For instance, in a movie about Martin Luther King, the casting agency can legitimately require applicants to be black men.

However, in questionable cases, the employer must show that the qualifications are reasonably necessary for the performance of a particular job.

Asking the same questions, for example, "Are you married" Do you have children?" to both men and women applicants does not mean that it is not a discriminatory question. The answer has different implications for women than for men.

Utah's Anti-Discrimination Act does not specifically list improper questions, but questions designed to elicit information about race, creed, sex, color, ancestry, or national origin are improper. For instance, questions about proof of birthplace which would reveal national origin or requests for photographs (which would reveal race) should be made *after* hiring.

CAN I BE DENIED A PROMOTION OR FIRED BECAUSE I AM PREGNANT?

Not if it is merely because you are pregnant. The basic principle of the Pregnancy Discrimination Act, 1978 amendment of Title VII, is that women affected by pregnancy and related conditions must be treated the same as other applicants and employees on the basis of their actual ability or inability to work.

You cannot be fired, or refused a job or promotion, merely because you are pregnant or have had an abortion. You cannot be forced to go on maternity leave as long as you can still work. You cannot be prevented from returning to work after maternity leave if other employees entitled to disability leave are entitled to get their jobs back. You cannot be denied disability benefits or sick leave if other employees who are unable to work for medical reasons get benefits or leave. If the employer had time requirements or could prove business necessity, employment could be denied. Remember, the burden of proof rests with the employer to prove such business necessity.

CAN AN EMPLOYER FIRE ME OR REFUSE TO HIRE ME BECAUSE OF MY SEXUAL PREFERENCE?

Sometimes. None of the many bills that have been introduced in Congress to outlaw discrimination against homosexuals have passed. Title VII's ban on discrimination based on sex is directed toward gender, not sexual practices and preferences.[1] This means that it is not illegal for someone to refuse to hire you if you are gay, or to fire you.

Cities may pass ordinances prohibiting employment discrimination against homosexuals, but there are no such ordinances in effect in Utah at this time.

WHAT IF I THINK I'M BEING DISCRIMINATED AGAINST FOR RELIGIOUS REASONS?

Your employer must "reasonably accommodate" your religious beliefs, practices, or observances when they conflict with your job-related duties. However, your employer need not make accommodations that would impose an "undue hardship" on the conduct of his or her business. For example, if two employees required Saturday off to observe their Sabbath, their employer would have the right to fire one of them and hire someone new if the job is so necessary that actual harm to the business would result if the job were not done.

DOES TITLE VII APPLY TO UNUSUAL RELIGIOUS AND TO INDIVIDUAL BELIEFS?

Generally, yes. Title VII gives a broad definition to the phrase "religious belief." It is not confined to traditional religious views, but includes ethical and moral beliefs that are sincerely held with the strength of traditional religious views.

WHAT DOES "NATIONAL ORIGIN" MEAN?

The Equal Employment Opportunity Commission (EEOC) defines "national origin" discrimination broadly as including, but not limited to, denying you equal employment opportunity because of your personal or ancestral place of origin or because you have the physical, cultural, or linguistic characteristics of a national group. For example, Hispanics are defined as individuals in this classification.

EEOC considers height and weight requirements as "suspect" if they tend to exclude individuals on the basis of national origin.

IF I FEEL I'M BEING DISCRIMINATED AGAINST IN EMPLOYMENT, HOW AND WHERE CAN I FILE A COMPLAINT?

In Utah, any person who is an employee or potential employee where twenty-five or more are employed (fifteen in federal offices), may file a complaint of discrimination because of race, color, sex, age, religion, ancestry, national origin, or handicap with the Utah Anti-Discrimination Division, Utah Industrial Commission, 160 East 300 South, Salt Lake City, Utah 84110-5800, telephone (801) 530-6922 or see listing under "Utah State Government," Industrial Commission of Utah. This office also accepts complaints from groups.

You may make complaints in person or in writing, but not over the phone.

DOES IT MATTER IF I SUBMIT A COMPLAINT AT THE UTAH ANTI-DISCRIMINATION OR THE EEOC?

If you are a federal employee or employed by a federal contractor, you should submit your complaint to the EEOC.

Utah Anti-Discrimination Division handles cases involving companies with at least twenty-five employees, employment agencies, labor organizations, joint apprenticeship committees, and vocational schools.

The Anti-Discrimination Act excludes federal agencies; religious organizations, associations, and corporations; and bona fide private membership clubs.

You must file charges of discrimination within thirty days from the time of alleged discrimination.

The Utah Anti-Discrimination Division (UADD) has a work-share agreement with EEOC and is authorized to accept complaints outside of its jurisdiction but covered under the statutes administered by EEOC. For example, the UADD could accept charges filed after the thirty days required by Utah's Anti-Discrimination Act, but before the EEOC's time limit of 180 days; charges filed against employers with between fifteen and twenty-five employees; or charges filed against employers with between twenty and fewer than twenty-five employees if it's a case of age discrimination.

WHAT IF I WORK FOR THE GOVERNMENT?

If you're a federal employee or employee of federal contractors you must file with their own agency.

You have thirty days to make an appointment and meet with an Equal Employment Opportunity counselor designated within your agency. Each agency should have one. That counselor will make an informal inquiry. After twenty-one days or after your final interview with the EEO counselor, you will be notified of what steps to make to pursue your complaint if nothing has been resolved. Within fifteen days after notification, you are required to make a formal written complaint.

The agency will hold an investigation and, based on the investigative record, make a recommendation. If you disagree with the recommendation, you are given a limited number of days to file a request for a hearing with the Equal Employment Opportunity Commission.

The EEOC will conduct a fact-finding hearing and an investigation of probable cause will be determined.

WHAT KIND OF INFORMATION DO I NEED WHEN I FILE A COMPLAINT?

The forms ask for your name, address, and telephone number; the name and address of the alleged violator (person, employer, employment agency, labor organization, joint apprenticeship committee, or vocational school); the specified practice you object to; and how you have been harmed.

The charge should have sufficient information to identify the unlawful practice, to identify the parties involved in the practice, to describe generally the action or practices complained of, and the harm such practice has had on you. You should have clearly in mind the remedy you are seeking. Do you want to be rehired? Do you want only back pay?

It is important to file your charge as soon as possible. Any award for back wages is limited to two years prior to the date on which you filed. Your records will be kept confidential, but the employer will be notified of your charges.

WHAT DO I HAVE TO DO TO PROVE THAT I HAVE BEEN DISCRIMINATED AGAINST?

Employment discrimination cases use two concepts of identifying unfair treatment:

1. Disparate treatment. In these cases, the employer simply treats some people less favorably than others because of their race, color, religion, sex, national origin, or age—for example, women are not considered for promotions to managerial levels.
2. Disparate impact. The employer's practices look neutral; but, in reality, they fall more harshly on one group than another and cannot be justified by business necessity.

WHAT HAPPENS AFTER I FILE MY CHARGE WITH THE ANTI-DISCRIMINATION DIVISION?

Your employer gets a copy and is asked to respond within ten days. After the employer submits this report, UADD holds a fact-finding conference with you and your employer. If you can't settle it then, UADD appoints an investigator to collect more information. At the end of the investigation the UADD investigator drafts a determination of cause or no cause, meaning there is cause for complaint or no cause.

HOW DO I BRING SUIT IN AN EMPLOYER DISCRIMINATION ACTION?

You have to file within certain time limits. In the case of age discrimination, you must wait thirty days before you can file. In the case of Title VII complaints, you may file 180 days after you have made your written complaint. The Industrial Commission allows thirty days after the final decision is made on the complaint.

It is best to consult either the Anti-Discrimination Division or EEOC on the matter and to seek legal counsel.

I FILED A COMPLAINT OF DISCRIMINATION AND MY BOSS IS MAKING THINGS HARD FOR ME. WHAT CAN I DO?

Whether you file with the UADD or with EEOC, you need to know that reprisals and harassment are unlawful. You have the option of filing a second charge of retaliation against the harassing employer or employees. The employer will then be notified of the second charge you have filed.

WHAT SHOULD I DO IF A UNION HAS DISCRIMINATED AGAINST ME?

If you are represented by a labor union that has fifteen or more members, you are probably protected against union discrimination by the Utah Anti-Discrimination Act, Title VII, and may follow these procedures we've just described.

You may also seek redress by the procedures of the National Labor Relations Act (NLRA).

Discrimination by a union is considered to be an "unfair labor practice" which is a violation of the NLRA.

8 Education

WHAT IS THE LEGAL STATUS OF WOMEN CONCERNING EDUCATION?

Traditionally, education has been a recognized and effective way for individuals to change their economic and social circumstances. Just as education can be the key to improving the quality of life, barriers to education can lock doors, preventing educational and economic opportunities. Therefore, equal access to and opportunity in education is a critical issue for Utah women.

Often those seeking to change existing prejudices and customs have met with hostility and ridicule. Many of the legal, social, political, and economic rights women enjoy and accept so naturally today were won by early day and modern pioneers sometimes at great personal costs.

Until recently, sex discrimination in education was largely ignored, unchallenged, and unchecked. Indeed such discrimination against women in the educational community was not illegal.

The Ninety-Second Congress, enacted a national policy that placed in motion the mechanism to end discrimination. The Equal Pay act of 1963, effective in 1964, amended the Fair Labor Standards Act to require that men and women performing equal work must receive equal pay. Title VII of the Civil Rights Act of 1964 was amended in 1972 to prohibit discrimination on the basis of sex in all administrative, executive, and professional employment practices in education, as well as in employment. In the same year Title IX of the Education Amendments of 1972 passed, prohibiting sex discrimination against students and employees in federally assisted educational programs. Subsequently, other interpretive guidelines have been issued that make sexual harassment illegal under Title VII of the Civil Rights Act of 1964 and Title IX of the Education Amendments of 1972 as amended. Another important source of help to women experiencing job discrim-

Table 1

SUMMARY OF FEDERAL STATUTES PROHIBITING DISCRIMINATION

Basis of Prohibited Discrimination	Area	Agency*	Statute
Race, color, religion, national origin, or sex	Employment	EEOC	Title VII, Civil Rights Act of 1964, as amended by the Equal Opportunity Act of 1972
Race, color, or national origin	Programs or activities	OCR/ED**	Title VI, Civil Rights Act of 1964
Sex	Employment programs or activities	OCR/ED**	Title IX, Civil Rights Act of 1964, Education Ammendments of 1972
Age (40-70)	Employment	EEOC	Age Discrimination in Employment Act of 1967, as amended
Age (does not limit coverage)	Programs or activities	OCR/ED**	Section 303, Age Discrimination Act of 1975
Handicap	Employment	OFCCP	Section 503 of the Rehabilitation Act of 1973, as amended
Handicap	Employment, programs or activities	OCR/ED**	Section 504 of the Rehabilitation Act of 1973, as amended
Veterans	Employment	OFCCP	38 USC 2011-2014, Vietnam Era Veterans Readjustment Assistance Act of 1974
Affirmative Action	Employment	OFCCP	Executive Order #11246, as amended
Equal Pay (Sex)	Employment	EEOC	Equal Pay Act of 1963

* External Enforcement Agency	Initials
Equal Employment Opportunity Commission	EEOC
Office of Civil Rights, Department of Education	OCR/ED
Office of Federal Contract Compliance Programs, Department of Labor	OFCCP/DOL

** or agency funding project

ination in education because of sex is not a law passed by Congress, but rather Executive Order 11246, issued by the President of the United States. Forbidding discrimination against minorities in employment, it was signed by President Lyndon B. Johnson in 1965, amended by Executive Order 11375 effective in 1968 to include a ban on discrimination because of sex.

Other legislation has been enacted to protect women from discrimination in employment, in education, and in access to educational programs and activities. These include: The Age Discrimination Act, Pregnancy Discrimination Act, and Sections 503 and 504 of the Rehabilitation Act of 1973.

WHAT IS SEX DISCRIMINATION?

Sex discrimination is any action that denies a person opportunities, privileges, roles, or rewards on the basis of his or her sex.

HOW CAN I RECOGNIZE SEX DISCRIMINATION?

Look for instances in which women or men are treated differently just because of their sex. See how they are hurt by being treated differently.

As a check, ask yourself a couple of questions:

—Am I being treated differently from students/teachers of the opposite sex?

—Am I experiencing any barriers due to differential treatment on the basis of sex?

If your answer is yes, you've most likely encountered some form of sex bias or discrimination.

WHAT IS TITLE VII?

Title VII of the Civil Rights Act, as we have said, prohibits discrimination in employment including education on the basis of race, color, religion, national origin, or sex. All institutions or agencies with fifteen or more employees, including state and local governments and labor organizations, are covered under the amended act. Title VII prohibits discriminatory practices in all terms and conditions of employment including:

—recruitment, selection, assignment, transfer, layoff, discharge, and recall

—opportunities for promotion

—in-service training or development opportunities

—wages and salaries

—sick leave time and pay

—vacation time and pay

—overtime work and pay

—medical, hospital, life, and accident insurance

—retirement plans and benefits

—other staff benefits

The enforcement agency is the Equal Employment Opportunity Commission.

WHAT IS EXECUTIVE ORDER 11246?

Executive Order 11246 addresses nondiscrimination under federal contract in two major areas:

Affirmative action must be taken to ensure that students and/or applicants are employed and are treated after employment without regard for race, creed, color, religion, national origin, sex, or age. Affirmative action further requires the employer to make additional efforts to recruit, employ, and promote qualified members of minority groups formerly excluded.

Nondiscrimination requires the elimination of all prohibited discriminatory conditions.

Under Executive Order 11246 discrimination in employment is prohibited in:

—employment, upgrading, demotion, or transfer
—recruitment or recruitment advertising
—layoffs or termination
—rates of pay or other forms of compensation
—selection for training, including apprenticeship

Unless positive action is taken to overcome the effects of systematic forms of discrimination, federal funds can be denied.

The Office of Federal Contract Compliance (OFCCP) enforces this order.

WHAT IS TITLE IX OF THE EDUCATION AMENDMENTS OF 1972?

Title IX of the Education Amendments of 1972 is a federal law designed to eliminate discrimination in educational programs and activities on the basis of sex. All institutions receiving federal funds are required to comply with the law in the admission and treatment of their students.

Title IX prohibits discrimination on the basis of sex in:

—admissions to vocational, graduate, professional and public undergraduate schools
—access to courses and programs
—counseling and guidance
—tests, materials, and practices
—physical education and athletics
—vocational education programs
—student rules and policies
—financial assistance (including student employment)
—student housing

—extracurricular activities
—employment in education institutions
—activities of enrolled students, including academic, extracurricular, and research activities
—career development and placement services
—health services
—conditions related to pregnancy (such disabilities are to be treated the same as any other temporary disability)

The enforcement agency of these amendments is the Office for Civil Rights/Equal Opportunity or the agency funding the project.

WHAT IS THE EQUAL PAY ACT OF 1963?

The Equal Pay Act prohibits unequal pay for men and women who work in the same establishment and on jobs requiring equal skill, effort, and responsibility which are performed under the same working conditions.

The Equal Pay Act prohibits discrimination on the basis of sex in:

—wages and fringe benefits
—sick and vacation leave
—health and life insurance
—pensions
—credit union benefits
—other retirement benefits based on sex

The Equal Employment Opportunity Commission enforces this act.

WHAT IS AGE DISCRIMINATION?

The Age Discrimination Act of 1967 (employment) and the Age Discrimination Act of 1975 (programs or activities), as amended, are designed to prohibit discrimination on the basis of age in employment and in programs or activities receiving federal financial assistance. Any employment decision relative to a person between the ages of forty and seventy must be based on the individual's ability or capacity to perform the work in question. The Equal Employment Opportunity Commission enforces these acts.

WHAT IS THE PREGNANCY DISCRIMINATION ACT?

The Pregnancy Discrimination Act, which became law in April 1979, prohibits discrimination on the basis of pregnancy, childbirth, or related medical conditions. The act does not require employers to provide special benefits for pregnant employees or to institute new programs. It simply requires that women affected by pregnancy be treated the same for all employment-related purposes as other persons not so affected but similar in their ability or inability to work.

The Pregnancy Discrimination Act prohibits an employer from treating pregnancy different than any other medical problem. An employer:

—Cannot refuse to hire a woman because she is pregnant.

—Can continue with any procedure used to determine the ability of all employees to work, such as a doctor's statement or examination as long as pregnancy-related conditions aren't singled out.

—Must make accommodations for pregnant workers similar to other temporarily disabled employees.

—Must hold the employee's job open for her in the same way used for employees on sick or disability leave unless the employee on leave has informed the employer that she doesn't intend to return to work.

WHAT IS SEXUAL HARASSMENT?

Unwelcome sexual advances, requests for sexual favors, and other verbal or physical conduct of a sexual nature constitute sexual harassment when:

— Submission to such conduct is made either explicitly or implicitly a term or condition of an individual's employment.

— Submission to or rejection of such conduct by an individual is used as the basis for employment decisions affecting such individual.

— Such conduct has the purpose or effect of unreasonably interfering with an individual's work performance or creating an intimidating, hostile, or offensive working environment.

Sexual Harassment is prohibited by Title VII of the Civil Rights Act of 1964 and Title IX of the Education Amendments of 1972.

HOW CAN I RECOGNIZE SEXUAL HARASSMENT?

Sexual harassment may range from sexual innuendos made at inappropriate times, perhaps in the guise of humor, to coerced sexual relations. It includes unwelcome and unwanted action such as:

—verbal harassment or abuse

—subtle pressure for sexual activity

—sexist remarks about a person's clothing, or body or sexual activities

—unnecessary touching, patting, or pinching

—constant brushing against a person's body

—demanding sexual favors accompanied by implied or overt threats concerning one's job, promotions, transfers, etc.

—physical assault (attempted rape or rape)

—leering or ogling of a person's body

Title VII is enforced by the Equal Employment Opportunity Commission, while the Office for Civil Rights/Equal Opportunity enforces Title IX.

WHAT IS TITLE VI OF THE CIVIL RIGHTS ACT OF 1964?

Title VI of the Civil Rights Act of 1964 provides that no person in the United States will, on the grounds, of race, color, or national origin, be excluded from participation in, be denied the benefits of, or be subjected to discrimination under any program or activity receiving federal financial assistance.

Responsibility for enforcement of Title VI rests with the Department of Education (formerly HEW), which has the power to withhold federal funds from any educational institution which practices discrimination based on race, color, or national origin.

Title VI prohibits discrimination on the basis of race, color, or national origin. It is illegal to:

—deny an individual any service, financial aid, or other benefit which is provided in a different manner from that provided to other individuals under the program.

—subject an individual to segregation or separate treatment in any matter related to his or her receipt of any service, financial aid, or other benefit under the program.

—restrict an individual in any way in the enjoyment of any advantage or privilege enjoyed by others receiving any service, financial aid, or other benefit under the program.

—treat an individual differently from others in determining whether he or she satisfies any admission, enrollment, quota, eligibility, membership, or other requirement or condition which individuals must meet to receive any service, financial aid, or other benefit provided under the program.

—deny a person the opportunity to participate as a member of a planning or advisory body which is an integral part of the program.

HOW DOES TITLE VI AFFECT MINORITY WOMEN?

Minority women may be subjected to double discrimination—discriminated against because of both her race and sex. If double discrimination occurs, a woman could pursue legal recourse under both Title VI on the basis of race and other applicable acts through the Office of Civil Rights/Equal Opportunity.

WHAT ARE THE SECTIONS 503 *and* 504 OF THE REHABILITATION ACT OF 1973?

Section 503 (employment) and Section 504 (programs and activities) of the Rehabilitation Act of 1973 are designed to eliminate discrimination on the basis of handicap in any program including education receiving federal financial assistance.

An institution may not, in providing any employment, aid, benefit, or service, on the basis of handicap:

—deny a qualified, handicapped person employment or the opportunity to participate in or benefit from any aid, benefit, or service.

—offer a qualified, handicapped person employment or an opportunity to participate in or benefit from any aid, benefit, or service that is not equal to that afforded others.

—provide a qualified, handicapped person with an aid, benefit, or service that is not as effective as that provided to others.

—provide different or separate aid, benefits, or services to handicapped persons or to any class of handicapped person with an aid, benefit, or service that is not as effective as that provided to others.

—perpetuate discrimination against a qualified, handicapped person by providing significant assistance to an agency, organization, or person that discriminates on the basis of handicap in providing any employment, aid, benefit, or service to beneficiaries of any program.

—deny a qualified, handicapped person the opportunity to participate as a member of planning or advisory boards.

—limit a qualified, handicapped person in his or her employment or in the enjoyment of any right, privilege, advantage, or opportunity enjoyed by others receiving an aid, benefit or service.

WHAT IS THE DEFINITION OF "HANDICAPPED"?

Section 504 of the Rehabilitation Act of 1973 defines *handicapped* as "any person who (1) has a physical or mental impairment which substantially limits one or more of such person's major life activities, (2) has a record of such an impairment, or (3) is regarded as having such an impairment."

Under this definition, *handicapped* can encompass any individual who is confined to a wheelchair, blind, alcoholic or formerly alcoholic, addicted or formerly addicted to drugs, epileptic, diabetic, mentally impaired, or directly affected or limited in his or her major life activities, whether or not the condition is hidden.

Accessibility is a major part of Section 504. All handicapped individuals should have access to all programs and/or buildings, classrooms, and facilities on the campus. At present, every effort is being made to make all buildings and facilities accessible for all individuals. The Equal Opportunity Office should be notified of any area or program on campus that is not accessible to everyone.

The Office of Federal Contract Compliance enforces Section 503, the OFCCP and the OCR/EO enforces program equality.

WHAT IS THE VIETNAM ERA VETERANS' READJUSTMENT ACT OF 1974?

This act requires an institution to take affirmative action to employ and advance in employment disability veterans and veterans of the Vietnam era.

It is illegal for an educational institution to discriminate against any employee or applicant for employment because he or she is a disabled veteran or veteran of the Vietnam era in regard to any position for which the employee or applicant for employment is qualified. An institution must:

—take affirmative action to employ and advance in employment qualified, disabled veterans, and veterans of the Vietnam era without discrimination based upon their disabilities or veterans' status.

—treat qualified, disabled veterans and veterans of the Vietnam era without discrimination based upon their disabilities or veterans' status in all employment practices, such as (1) employment, upgrading, demotion, or transfer, (2) recruitment and advertising, (3) layoff or termination, (4) rates of pay or other forms of compensation, or (5) selection for training, including apprenticeship.

This act's enforcement agency is the Office of Federal Contract Compliance.

BEFORE I FILE A COMPLAINT WHAT DO I NEED TO CONSIDER?

If you feel that you have been discriminated against you need to:

—try to resolve the complaint informally at the lowest level, i.e., supervisor, teacher, principal, etc., or discuss the concern with the grievance officer or a knowledgeable person.

—request that your conversation or inquiry be kept confidential.

—provide receipts, contacts, or other records supporting your claim of discrimination.

—identify witnesses who have information regarding your claim.

—determine what you want to have happen to remedy the claim, i.e., back pay, promotion, transfer, grade change, access to programs and activities, etc.

If you decide to file a complaint alleging discrimination it is important to look carefully at the risks and trade-offs that are part of such a decision. By filing a complaint, you run the risk of alienating those you file the claim against and others in the system. Although the grievance procedure should be viewed as a means to resolve problems in a fair and equitable manner, it is often perceived as a confrontive course of action. Be prepared for the emotional cost often inherent in pursuing such a course of action.

HOW DO I FILE A COMPLAINT?

In any grievance or complaint, it is important to start with those processes available to you within the institution. When those options have been exhausted, you can then move to external remedies.

You are responsible for documenting the discrimination that happened to you. As soon as you feel you are experiencing discrimination (even if you're not sure) begin to keep a record of what takes place. Include such information as: day, complete date, time, place, names of those present, what exactly was said and who said what, what actions took place (verbal or physical threats), names of people who have experienced similar discrimination, copies of correspondence, or any other pertinent documents.

If time has passed and you have not been documenting what has been going on, then start immediately to reconstruct what has happened. Include everything you can that is related to your case. Do not personally censor what you deem to be important. Only someone specifically trained can make that determination. Something you feel is unimportant may be important as documentation to support your complaint.

HOW DO I FILE AN INTERNAL COMPLAINT?

Internal complaints refer to complaints filed within the institution where the alleged discrimination occurred. The following procedures should be followed when filing an internal complaint:

—Determine the appropriate office or individual to obtain information from about the internal grievance and/or appeals process within the institution.

—Determine the timelines/deadlines for filing the complaint. Timelines vary with each institution.

—Take action according to the institutional policies.

HOW DO I FILE AN EXTERNAL COMPLAINT?

External complaints refer to complaints filed with the appropriate federal and/or state agency against an institution for alleged discrimination. There are specific federal and state agencies responsible for enforcement of the various laws depending on the basis of the alleged discrimination. To determine the basis of the prohibited discrimination and the agency responsible for enforcement of the specific law refer to Table 1. If you decide to file a complaint it must be done within 180 days of the alleged violation. Following are the addresses and phone numbers of the enforcement agencies to contact when filing an external complaint.

Utah Anti-Discrimination Division (UADD)
Industrial Commission
160 South 300 East
Salt Lake City, UT 84145-0580
Telephone: (801) 530-6922
or
Equal Employment Opportunity Commission (EEOC)
135 North 2nd Avenue
Phoenix, AZ 85003
Telephone: (602) 261-3882

Office of Federal Contract Compliance Programs (OFCCP)
125 South State, Suite 4221
Salt Lake City, UT 84138
Telephone: (801) 524-4470

Office for Civil Rights
Region VIII
U.S. Department of Education
1961 Stout St.
Denver, CO 80294
Telephone: (303) 844-4957

9 Mental and Physical Health

Mental Health

WHAT IS MENTAL HEALTH?

Like physical health, mental "health" is a very broad term that covers many shades of well-being and can be influenced by many different factors: diet, exercise, or stress, among them. The President's Commission on Mental Health (1978) estimated that up to 15 percent of Americans may experience mental health problems.

Mental health is often defined as the absence of any identifiable or significant mental disorder. Most definitions describe a mentally healthy person as one who feels comfortable about herself, interacts harmoniously with others, functions constructively in social and physical situations, and meets personal and societal needs without undue stress. This sense of well-being is an important part of your general good health.

If you have a psychiatric disorder which significantly impairs your mental, emotional, or behavioral functioning, then the community has an interest in seeing that you do not injure yourself or others. In so doing, it interacts with you in a way that involves your legal rights. Some serious disorders include organic brain syndrome, schizophrenia, and depression. Mental illness can also involve the less serious but still troubling aspects of marital or sexual conflicts, learning problems, and self-image problems.

WHAT KINDS OF HELP CAN I GET IF I AM MENTALLY ILL?

Mental health services cover an immense range of facilities and treatments. Historically, families cared for mentally ill members. Then, beginning during the eighteenth and nineteenth centuries, the care of the mentally ill gradually became the exclusive responsibility of large institutions. This condition lasted until the 1950s and 1960s.

More community-based services became available. Today there are increasing numbers of outpatient clinics, general hospitals with inpatient units for psychiatric patients, and nursing homes that care for the aged chronic mental patient.[1] In 1986, Utah will have several private psychiatric hospitals.

Some of these changes came about because of the introduction of major tranquilizers and psychoactive drugs. Even severely psychotic patients did not need to be physically institutionalized all the time. Treatment innovations emphasize a continuum of care from intensive treatment for the acutely ill to community-based aftercare programs.

The type of mental health problem you have will help determine the services you receive. The Utah Health Systems Agency has broadly categorized mental health service as follows:

1. *Crisis Intervention Services* focus on controlling and helping disabilities so that you won't hurt yourself or someone else. Services may include chemotherapy, emergency intervention, therapy with significant others, etc.
2. *Rehabilitation Services* work with people who are in no immediate danger but who aren't able to fully care for themselves. A schizophrenic is an example of someone with chronic mental disabilities. Services consist of occupational therapy, medication maintenance, recreation, vocational training, and self-care skills.
3. *Prevention Services* are designed to prevent future problems by helping you acquire the interpersonal and working skills to get along better as an individual, couple, and with your family. It also tries to help you be successful at finding and keeping a job.

TYPES OF MENTAL HEALTH SETTINGS

Hospitals

Settings
- State Mental Hospital
- General hospitals
  - Medical beds
  - Designated psychiatric
  - Outpatient clinics
  - Emergency rooms
- Veterans Administration
- Private psychiatric hospitals

Residential Facilities
- Nursing homes
- Boarding homes
- Group homes, halfway houses
- Adult foster homes
- Subsidized cooperative living
- Residential treatment facilities for children
- Private residences
- Homes of relatives or friends

Criminal Justice System Settings
- Medical units in jails and prisons
- General jail or prison facilities
- Juvenile detention facilities
- Probation and parole
- Law enforcement offices
- Criminal and sexual offender units and the State Hospital

Private Outpatient
- Specialists in mental health: psychiatrists, psychologists, social workers, psychiatric nurses
- Medical professionals: general physicians, family physicians,osteopaths, internists

Pastoral counselors, marriage and family counselors, school counselors

Private mental health clinics

Public Community-Based Settings
- Social Service Settings:
  - Child protection agencies
  - Schools
  - Youth services systems
  - Church social services
  - Juvenile Courts
  - Crisis, information, and referral centers
  - Other health and social services
- Mental Health Agencies:

Comprehensive community mental health centers *including inpatient facilities*

Outpatient mental health clinics

Day treatment facilities
- Self-help groups and alternative mental health practitioners

Services consist of vocational guidance, psychotherapy, and group therapy.

WHERE CAN I GO FOR HELP IF I AM MENTALLY ILL?

The Utah Health Systems Agency has made a chart listing the various types of places you can get mental health treatment. Some are publicly funded and others are private.

The Utah Health Systems Agency has described and defined some of these major settings.

Psychiatric hospital: This is a public or private hospital in which the primary concern is to provide inpatient psychiatric care to mentally ill persons. The Utah State Hospital is located in Provo.

General hospital with a psychiatric unit: This is a general, short-term, acute-care hospital that provides a wide variety of types of health care, including psychiatric care in a designated unit. In Utah these facilities have a set number of beds specifically for use by psychiatric patients. A psychiatric unit provides a variety of services, including emergency care, in-patient services, and day care. Almost all general hospitals accept psychiatric patients for short-term crisis care.

Mental Health Center: Comprehensive Mental Health Centers (CMHCs) are programs that were set up by federal law in 1963[2] to provide a comprehensive array of services to meet the varying demands of the people within the areas that they serve. CMHCs are a federal, state, and local partnership. Their services include community-based inpatient care; partial care; out-patient care; emergency care; consultation and education; transitional care or residential treatment; children's services; services for the aged, or alcohol and drug abusers; and screening and follow-up care for institutionalized patients. There are also Community Mental Health Centers which do not have federal sponsorship. These are usually county-wide or multi-county service offices.

Residential Treatment Center: This is a structured twenty-four-hour care facility that provides treatment services to people who are clinically diagnosed as being mentally or emotionally disabled. Licensed professional nursing services are not provided in such a residence, but assistance and supervision in the activities of daily living are available.

Long-Term Care Facility: Long-term care facilities offer a residential service setting with nursing care to many mentally ill patients. Local community mental health centers provide care for a majority of these patients. Such facilities may be categorized by the level of nursing care, intermediate or skilled.

Day Treatment Services: This type of partial care provides planned therapeutic programs to people who require less than twenty-four-hour care, yet who can benefit from more than is available in an outpatient clinic setting. Some examples of partial care programs are: Day/Evening Care and Sheltered Workshops. A mentally handicapped person would receive supervision in what is basically an independent and transitional living arrangement.

Private Practitioner: The private practitioner provides community-based mental health care to a wide range of clients who are both publicly and privately financed. Professionals within this group include psychiatrists, psychologists, psychiatric social workers, psychiatric nurses, marriage and family counselors, educational counselors, and other specially trained practitioners.

Locations:

To find these facilities and people, check your local telephone directory under "hospital," "mental health," and "counselors."

HOW MUCH WILL IT COST?

The cost of mental health care varies widely according to the treatment setting. Of course, hospitalization costs more than outpatient therapy. Generally speaking, private settings cost more than public or community-based settings. All mental health programs, public or private, charge fees for their services. However, if you cannot afford care, you may be eligible for reduced rates through your local Community Mental Health Center. State law prohibits refusing services to you because of your inability to pay.[3] If hospitalization is required, the state of Utah can collect money from Medicaid or any Social Security disability benefits you may qualify for to help pay costs of care.

It is your right as a mental health care consumer to ask for and receive information about costs of treatment, methods of payment, and medical assistance funding programs for which you may qualify.

WHAT IF I HAVE TO GO TO THE HOSPITAL?

If a mental health professional determines that hospitalization is required, you may be admitted to a local hospital with designated psychiatric beds.

You may also be referred to the Utah State Hospital. The Utah State Hospital in Provo functions under the Division of Mental Health in the Utah State Department of Social Services. It provides services to individuals with such severe chronic problems that there are few or no community-based treatment alternatives. In most cases, they are too dangerous or difficult to manage for the community. The mentally retarded are cared for separately and may be admitted to the Utah State Training School.[4]

Minors under age sixteen may be admitted to the State Hospital if their parent or legal guardian applies in their behalf.[5]

The State Hospital is licensed for 338 beds and has an average of 1.5 full-time equivalent staff per patient (a ratio equivalent to the national norm). The following patient populations are served: geriatric, forensic, neurologically impaired, chronic severely emotionally disturbed, drug, alcohol, and emotionally disturbed children and youth.

WHAT IF I AM TOO SICK TO DECIDE WHAT TO DO?

If you are too sick to choose for yourself to seek treatment, then someone else may take you to a mental health facility or hospital. The staff of the facility will decide what level of care is necessary and whether to admit you for hospitalization. If a mental health professional determines that you are too disoriented to be responsible for your own health and safety, then the staff may arrange for an "involuntary admission" to the facility. The important difference between voluntary and involuntary admission is that if you are voluntarily admitted, you may leave the hospital at any time. You cannot be detained against your will unless hospital clinical personnel have decided you might harm yourself or others or if legal involuntary hospitalization proceedings have been started.[6]

HOW DOES INVOLUNTARY ADMISSION OR COMMITMENT HAPPEN?

County mental health programs can hospitalize mental patients by court commitment. These admissions are involuntary. The Utah Code Annotated (1953; amended, 1979), Sections 64-7-32 and 36, describe the provisions for involuntary hospitalization.

A "responsible person" who knows about your circumstances, believes you are mentally ill, and thinks you should be involuntarily hospitalized must make a written application. A "responsible person" is usually a relative who has assumed responsibility for your care—a husband, your mother, or an adult child, for instance. This application must be accompanied by a certificate from a licensed physician or a state-designated examiner stating that he or she has examined you within the last seven days, believes that you are mentally ill, and recommends that you be involuntarily hospitalized. Or the responsible person must include a written statement that the patient has refused to submit to an examination of mental condition by a licensed physician or state-designated examiner.[7]

In addition to the court-ordered examination, you are entitled to a hearing where you may be represented by a lawyer. After this hearing, the judge will order hospitalization if five questions[8] are answered in the affirmative:

1. Do you have a mental illness?
2. Because of this illness, do you pose an "immediate danger of physical injury" to yourself or others? This "immediate danger" may be an inability to feed yourself or a dependent child, to stay on the sidewalk instead of blundering into traffic because you are disoriented, or being unable to perform other normal and necessary functions.
3. Do you lack the ability to carry out a rational decision-making process about your own treatment for mental illness? Are you unable, for instance, to weigh the pros and cons of treatment, decide whether the merits outnumber the costs, etc.? Are there no alternatives to a court order of hospitalization that are less restrictive and equally appropriate?
4. Will the hospital or mental health facility provide you with treatment appropriate and adequate to your condition?

If these five questions cannot be answered, the court will dismiss the involuntary hospitalization proceedings and you cannot be kept in the State Hospital or other mental health facility.

During these proceedings, you are given a chance to agree to become a voluntary patient, which means you would be free to leave at any time.

Placements of involuntarily admitted patients may occur in any designated mental health facility and are frequently made with the State Hospital. The detention period may be temporary (less than six months) or indeterminate. The tracking and treatment plan for patients who are court-committed is done by county mental health programs in conjunction with the State Division of Mental Health.

WHAT LEGAL RIGHTS DO I HAVE AFTER ADMISSION?

Admission to a hospital for mental health care does not mean you cannot make legal decisions. Unless the court finds you incapacitated, you can exercise all civil rights, including the right to dispose of property, write and sign contracts like a will or a mortgage, make purchases, and enter contractual relationships. You also may vote, marry, and drive a car.[9]

WHAT IS "INCAPACITATION?"

In a legal sense, an "incapacitated person" is anyone who is impaired by reason of mental illness, mental deficiency, physical illness or disability, advanced age, chronic use of drugs, chronic intoxication, or other causes (except youth) to the extent that he or she lacks sufficient understanding or capacity to make or communicate responsible decisions about his or her well-being.[10]

The allegedly incapacitated person or anyone interested in his or her welfare may ask the court for a finding of "incapacitation" and the appointment of a guardian who will provide care for the person.[11] A guardian determines where the incapacitated person lives, provides for the person's care and comfort, cares for the person's personal possessions, and can give medical consent for treatment of the incapacitated person if necessary.[12]

A finding of incapacitation and the appointment of a guardian does *not* mean that you are mentally ill or can be involuntarily hospitalized.[13] However, if you have been found mentally ill and involuntarily hospitalized, it may not be necessary to have additional court proceedings to appoint a guardian. The appointment of a guardian depends on the individual situation.

Where the incapacitated person cannot manage his or her property and financial affairs, someone may petition the court to appoint a conservator. A conservator is granted all legal power to manage the property and funds of the incapacitated person for his or her benefit.[14] Note that a conservator is granted power only over an incapacitated person's property, while a guardian has greater responsibility relating to the incapacitated person's personal care and well-being.

The incapacitated person or any other interested person may petition the court at any time to end the guardianship and/or conservatorship.[15]

WHAT WILL HAPPEN IN THE HOSPITAL?

The Utah Legislature has said that every patient is entitled to humane care and to medical care that follows the prevailing standards of medical practice, psychiatric nursing practice, social work practice, and the practice of clinical psychology.[16] In the hospital, the staff will develop a mental health treatment plan for you. You are the key to the success of the plan so you should ask questions about medications that are prescribed for you, how often you see your therapist, and so forth. If you have problems with a medication or a therapist, try to work the problem out with the staff. You have the right to refuse medication and to stop seeing your therapist. But if you are a voluntary patient and refuse all medicine and treatment, then the hospital staff may discharge you on the ground that you have refused the help they can offer you.

Every patient has the right to communicate by sealed mail or otherwise with persons inside or outside the hospital and to receive visitors.[17] Patients cannot be subjected to unnecessary mechanical restraint or medication.[18]

WILL MY THERAPIST TELL ANYONE WHAT I SHARE WITH HIM OR HER?

All health care professionals have ethical standards which require holding patient information in strict confidence. Your therapist will not reveal your secrets or confidences to your husband, parents, or children. In addition to ethical standards, there are legal standards requiring confidentiality. No one other than those treating you can see your medical record without your written consent. Legal penalties can be imposed against health care personnel and/or facilities for violating confidentiality requirements.[19]

WHAT IS ELECTROCONVULSIVE (SHOCK) THERAPY?

Electroconvulsive therapy, often called ECT or shock therapy, is a medical procedure by which carefully controlled amounts of electric current are passed through the brain. Some psychiatrists recommend ECT for some types of mental disorders, often for deep-seated depression which does not respond to other forms of therapy. ECT is a controversial treatment because of some of its possible side effects. You must sign a written consent to ETC acknowledging that your psychiatrist has informed you of the benefits, the risks, and side effects of ECT before you can receive ECT treatment.

WHAT IS A LOBOTOMY?

A lobotomy is a surgical procedure by which a particular portion of the brain which controls behavior is removed. Lobotomy is a drastic, last-resort procedure. Since the development of antipsychotic medications (in the 1950s and 1960s) to control violent psychotic behavior, lobotomies are very rarely performed.

Physical Health

DO I NEED A PRESCRIPTION FOR BIRTH CONTROL DEVICES?

If you want to use the pill, an IUD, or a diaphragm, you will need a prescription from a doctor. Other methods, such as condoms or foam, are available without a prescription. Your druggist can tell you which are and which aren't. The prescription methods are usually long-term, and one purpose of the law is to be sure you understand how to use them correctly and what possible side effects might be.

MUST I OBTAIN MY PARENTS' CONSENT FOR BIRTH CONTROL SERVICES? WILL MY PARENTS BE NOTIFIED?

Generally not, teenagers do not have to obtain their parents' consent to receive birth control services. However, Utah does require that you have the prior written consent of a parent or guardian to use any public funds (medical card, state or county health department services) to obtain contraceptives if you are an unmarried minor.[20]

If you are over eighteen or married, there are no restrictions on your right to obtain birth control services or contraceptives.

WHAT IS STERILIZATION?

Sterilization is a medical procedure or operation that will probably make it permanently impossible for you to have children. For men, the operation is a vasectomy. For women, it can either be a tubal ligation, a hysterectomy, the removal of ovaries, or a combination. A tubal ligation is the simplest, most common, the least expensive, and has the fewest side effects. It blocks the fallopian tubes which carry the eggs to the uterus. Tubal ligation is usually a contraceptive choice and is therefore elective surgery. Removing either the ovaries or the uterus is major surgery and is generally never used for contraceptive reasons. This surgery is used when medically indicated for reasons other than contraceptive and is rarely if ever elective. None of these operations should be done until you thoroughly discuss what kinds of surgical procedures are involved and what the long-term and short-term consequences will be.

WHAT ARE THE LEGAL CONDITIONS FOR STERILIZATION?

In 1983, the Utah legislature passed a law regulating the circumstances under which you or your partner may be sterilized.[21] This law provides that physicians may sterilize any person who meets three conditions: (1) is eighteen years of age or older; (2) voluntarily consents; and (3) is capable of understanding the nature and consequences of sterilization, and the available alternate methods of contraception.[22]

If you are under eighteen and you are married or not living with or dependent on your parents, you still may be sterilized if you meet the second two conditions.

The law also has special protection for people who want to be sterilized and who are institutionalized—meaning those living in the Utah State Training School, Utah State Hospital, a residential facility for handicapped persons, a group home for disabled persons, a nursing home, or a foster home. The physician who performs the sterilization is responsible to carefully examine and counsel the person desiring sterilization to be sure that he or she has not been coerced or improperly influenced to consent by reason of his or her institutionalization.[23]

CAN I BE STERILIZED WITHOUT MY CONSENT?

If you're capable of giving informed consent, you cannot be forced to undergo sterilization. However, a person who is incapable of giving informed consent can be sterilized if a court orders sterilization, whether or not he or she wants to be sterilized.

A parent, spouse, guardian, custodian, or other interested person may file a petition for a court order of sterilization.[24]

After the petition is filed, the court will appoint an attorney to represent the person to be sterilized.[25] At the hearing on the petition, the court will hear evidence regarding the person to be sterilized.[26]

The petition must prove beyond a reasonable doubt that the person will suffer serious physical or psychological injury if the sterilization is not performed.[27] The court must consider two questions before granting the petition: What is the best interest of the person to be sterilized? and What decision would this person make if he or she were capable of giving informed consent?[28]

The law on sterilization does not prohibit medical treatment for sound therapeutic reasons that incidentally involve the destruction of the reproductive functions.[29] For example, hysterectomies are often performed for medical reasons other than sterilization, such as to remove cancerous organs.

IS ABORTION LEGAL?

The famous Supreme Court decision in *Roe v. Wade*[30], handed down in 1973, still forms the bedrock of abortion law in this country. In *Roe v. Wade*, the Supreme Court held that the fundamental right of privacy includes a woman's right to decide whether to terminate her pregnancy. However, the court also held that balanced against a woman's right to privacy is the state's interest in protecting both the potentiality of human life and the mother's health. The Supreme Court broke the nine month term of pregnancy into three trimesters, giving the woman's right to privacy and the state's interest in protecting her health and that of the fetus different weights during each trimester. During the first trimester of pregnancy, the woman's right to choose whether to terminate her pregnancy is paramount over the state's interests and the state has little control over abortions. A licensed physician may perform abortions in his or her office.[31]

As the pregnancy progresses, the medical complications increase, and the state may intervene to protect the mother's health. During the second trimester, Utah has defined its interest in preserving the mother's health to mean that abortions must be performed in a hospital or clinic certified by the state.[32]

During the third trimester, when the fetus has a reasonable chance of surviving outside the mother's womb, the state may forbid abortions altogether except when necessary to save the life or health of the mother. Utah forbids abortions beginning with the seventh month except when necessary to save the mother's life or prevent serious and *permanent* damage to her health.[33]

MUST I NOTIFY MY HUSBAND OR PARENTS OF AN ABORTION?

There is no minimum age requirement for obtaining an abortion. However, Utah law requires the physician to notify your parents or guardian if you an "unemancipated" minor.[34] If you are under eighteen, but you are "emancipated"—that is married or not living with or dependent on your parents, you do not have to notify your parents or guardian of an abortion.[35]

Utah law requires the physician to notify your husband, if it is physically possible to do so.[36]

WILL MEDICAID PAY FOR AN ABORTION?

Medicaid will only pay for abortion in maternal life-endangering pregnancies. See *Jane Does v. State of Utah Dept. of Health*, 776 F.2d (10th Cir. 1985).

10 Women and Criminal Justice

WHAT DOES "CRIMINAL" MEAN IN A LEGAL SENSE?

When a person violates a penal statute she is considered to have committed a wrong against society as a whole instead of merely a personal wrong against the victim of the crime. Therefore crimes are prosecuted in the name of a governmental entity against the defendant. In the case of felony crimes, the title of the case would be "State of Utah vs. Joe Defendant." The victim does not prosecute. She becomes a witness for the prosecution. Persons who are convicted of crimes face potential penalties of both fines and periods of incarceration.

A civil case involves one private person or entity suing another. The title of a civil lawsuit would be "Jane Plaintiff vs. Joe Defendant." If the plaintiff prevails in a civil suit, she will receive a judgment for money damages against the defendant. Nobody is put in jail as a result of a civil lawsuit.

In a criminal case, the state always has the burden of proving that the defendant committed the crime "beyond a reasonable doubt." In a civil case, the plaintiff bears the lesser burden of proving the cause of action by "a preponderance of the evidence."

Crimes in the state of Utah are divided into several different categories of seriousness. Felonies, the more serious crimes, are divided into subcategories which include capital, first-degree, second-degree, and third-degree felonies. Misdemeanors are divided into the subcategories of class A, class B and class C misdemeanors.

WHAT IS SEXUAL ASSAULT?

A sexual assault is a crime of violence with a sexual component, committed against one person by another. The experts do not believe that sexual assaults are sexually motivated but rather are crimes of violence, motivated by anger, hatred, and the need to control and degrade women in the ultimate sense.

In 1983, the Utah State Legislature extensively revised Utah's sexual assault laws. Most of its work greatly strengthened the legal protection available to women and also created many separate categories of crimes upon children. The laws relevant to sexual assaults today are discussed below.

HOW IS "RAPE" DEFINED LEGALLY?

Utah law states that "a person commits rape when [he or she] has sexual intercourse with another person, not [his] spouse, without the victim's consent.[1] (The meaning of "consent" is discussed later.) Any penetration is sufficient to constitute the act of sexual intercourse.[2] Ejaculation is not required. Rape is a first-degree felony which is punishable by five years to life in the state prison and/or a fine of up to $10,000.

HOW DOES THE LAW DEFINE "RAPE OF A CHILD"?

"A person commits rape of a child when [he or she] has sexual intercourse with a child who is under the age of fourteen."[3] This crime may be committed regardless of the victim's consent. The law says that children under the age of fourteen years are legally incapable of consenting to sex acts.[4] Rape of a child is a first-degree felony carrying with it a mandatory prison sentence of at least five years unless the defendant is a parent of the victim and can prove to the court a series of mitigating factors.[5]

WHAT IS "UNLAWFUL SEXUAL INTERCOURSE"?

Unlawful sexual intercourse occurs when a man or a woman has sexual intercourse with a person under sixteen who is not his or her spouse.[6] Again, the victim's consent is irrelevant. This crime is a Class B misdemeanor punishable by up to six months in jail and a fine of up to $299, if the defendant is no more than three years older than the victim. If the defendant is more than three years older than the victim, it is a third-degree felony punishable by up to five years in prison and a fine of up to $5,000.[7]

WHAT IS "OBJECT RAPE"?

Utah law creates a separate crime for a rape which is committed with a foreign object or instrument which is not part of the human body. This crime is called object rape or object rape of a child if the victim is a child under the age of fourteen.[8] It is a first-degree felony punishable by up to life in prison and a fine of up to $10,000. Object rape of a child carries with it a prison sentence of at least five years.[9]

WHAT IS SODOMY?

Sodomy is defined as a sexual act involving the genitals of one person and the mouth or anus of another person.[10] Utah law creates three separate categories for sodomy: sodomy, forcible sodomy, and sodomy upon a child. Sodomy is punishable as a Class B misdemeanor regardless of the consent of the victim.[11] Forcible sodomy means the act is committed without the victim's consent and is a first-degree felony.[12] Sodomy upon a child means sodomy is committed upon a child under the age of fourteen. The consent of the child is irrelevant.[13] This crime is punishable as a first-degree felony and carries with it a mandatory prison sentence of at least five years.[14]

ARE HOMOSEXUAL ACTIVITIES PROHIBITED IN UTAH?

Utah's sodomy statute has been interpreted to prohibit sexual conduct between members of the same sex, although the statute does not say so explicitly. The United States Supreme Court has said this statute was constitutional when it was applied to homosexual activities between consenting adults in private.[15] Marriage to a person of the same sex is also prohibited under Utah law.[16]

WHAT IS FORCIBLE SEXUAL ABUSE OR SEXUAL ABUSE OF A CHILD?

Forcible sexual abuse is defined as a touching of the anus, buttocks, genitals or breasts, or otherwise taking indecent liberties with a victim over the age of fourteen without the consent of the victim.[17] The intent of the perpetrator must be to arouse or gratify the sexual desires of any person, including someone other than the child or the perpetrator, or to cause substantial emotional or bodily pain to any person.[18]

Sexual abuse of a child is the same crime committed upon a child under fourteen except that the consent of the victim is irrelevant.[19] Forcible sexual abuse and sexual abuse of a child are both second-degree felonies punishable by one to fifteen years in prison and a fine of up to $10,000.[20]

WHAT IS AGGRAVATED SEXUAL ASSAULT?

A person commits aggravated sexual assault if, in the course of committing one of the sex crimes described above, he or she causes bodily injury to the victim, uses a dangerous weapon, threatens the victim with kidnapping, death, or serious bodily injury, or is aided or abetted by one or more persons. Aggravated sexual assault is a first-degree felony and carries with it a mandatory prison sentence of least five years.[21]

In Utah, you are legally incapable of committing these crimes upon your own spouse. The conduct of married persons is exempt from the provisions of this part of the law.[22] However, if your husband rapes you, threatens you, or uses a foreign instrument, he can be charged with assault. If you are married but living apart by the terms of a court order, these laws apply as if you were not married.

WHAT DOES "CONSENT" MEAN?

The victim's lack of consent or agreement is a key element in crimes against victims fourteen years of age and older. The issue of consent is ultimately decided in each case by the judge or jury who tries a case. But the law does give some guidance on deciding when one of these acts has been committed without consent of the victim.

Generally, the act is considered to be without the victim's consent when:

1. The defendant "compels the victim to submit or participate by force that overcomes such earnest resistance as might reasonably be expected under the circumstances."
2. The defendant "compels the victim to submit or participate by any threat that would prevent resistance by a person of ordinary resolution."
3. The victim is unconscious or physically unable to resist or is mentally handicapped to the extent that she or he is incapable of understanding the nature of the act or of resisting it.
4. The victim is under the age of fourteen.[23]

Basically, the law requires only that a victim demonstrate her resistance and lack of consent in a way that is reasonable under the circumstances.

Some people believe rape is a crime of sexual passion. Research in psychology and criminology indicates it is more accurately described as an act of violence motivated not by passion but by hostility and rage.[24] It is a physical assault that results in mental agony for the victim, and, often, some degree of physical injury in the form of abrasions, contusions, disease, or infection. The possibility of an unwanted pregnancy would also be considered a negative consequence for the victim.

Rape is a brutal crime which could happen to any woman. The Salt Lake Rape Crisis Center has provided services to victims ranging in age from seven months to eighty-six years of age. Most victims are raped in their own homes by a person they trusted or knew to some degree.[25] It is estimated that someone is raped every six minutes in this country[26] so it is important for you to know what to do and what to expect in case of such an assault.

WHAT SHOULD I DO IF I'VE BEEN RAPED?

You have several choices. You may wish to call a friend, relative, or professional helper from the local Rape Crisis Center. (Your local center will be listed in your phone book.) The Rape Crisis Center in Salt Lake City can be reached twenty-four hours a day at 532-7274. You may want to call a doctor, go to a hospital emergency room and/or you can call the police.

SHOULD I REPORT MY RAPE TO THE POLICE?

The FBI says rape is the most under-reported crime in the United States.[27] Despite the sometimes unpleasant aspects of police questioning and a trial, you should remember that a report to the police is the way to stop the rapist from committing further assaults. Sex offenders rarely commit a single crime. In Utah, emphasis is placed on training police officers to handle sexual assault cases with kindness and consideration. The fears you may have about how you will be treated by the police probably no longer reflect reality. A great deal of progress has been made in this area recently.

You may report the rape anonymously to the police, without pressing charges, by having a rape crisis worker submit a "Third Party Report Form" for you. The report may help officers to identify the areas where rapes frequently occur, the patterns of the rapist, and perhaps the identity of the rapist. However, no legal action can be taken against the rapist unless you are willing to become involved. While the decision to report a rape is a personal one which you must make yourself, remember that it is not something you have to go through alone. Support is available through your local Rape Crisis Center.

If you decide to report the rape, you should call the police immediately. This will ensure as complete a collection of evidence as possible. If you feel comfortable with your doctor, you might choose to contact her/him as well.

WHAT SHOULD I DO WHILE WAITING FOR THE POLICE?

It is important to preserve as much evidence as possible against the man who raped you. Do not change your clothes, wash, bathe, douche, or clean your wounds immediately after the assault. If you do, you will destroy any physical evidence such as stains, hairs, or bodily fluids which may remain. Do not touch any surface the rapist touched to preserve his fingerprints. While details are fresh, it is important to write down whatever you remember about the rapist's description, his vehicle, and what direction he went when he left.

WHAT WILL THE POLICE ASK ME?

The police officer, who will frequently be a woman, will probably first be concerned about any medical help you need. Then he or she will want a complete description of the assailant. If the rape has just happened, this information will be broadcast on the police radio so patrol cars may begin to look for him. You will then be asked to describe the assault. At some point, you will also be questioned by a police detective about the assault. Some of the questions may seem intimate and embarrassing but complete information will help in apprehending the rapist and at the trial.

It is important to be completely honest with the officers. If you answer a question falsely, it can damage your credibility much more than any truthful answer could damage the case. You are entitled to courteous treatment by all police personnel; if you feel you have been treated otherwise, you should complain to the Internal Affairs Division of the police agency the officer works for. A police detective will take a formal complaint from you.

WILL I BE REQUIRED TO GO TO THE HOSPITAL?

If you report your rape to the police with the intention of prosecuting the rapist, the police will take you to the hospital emergency room for a medical exam. There are two purposes for this exam. First, your injuries will be treated and you will receive medication to prevent pregnancy and venereal disease. You will also have the opportunity to talk to the doctor about any medical concerns you may have.

The second purpose of the exam is to gather evidence against the man who raped you. Blood and urine samples along with vaginal, anal, and oral swabs will be taken. Your fingernails will be scraped and your pubic hair combed. All of these procedures are relatively painless. You are entitled to understand the reasons for these procedures and the hospital staff should be willing to answer any questions you may have. You should take a change of clothing with you to the hospital because the clothes you were wearing may need to be taken as evidence. You should not be charged for your initial hospital treatment. If you receive a bill, contact the police department you reported to and your county attorney's office. One of those agencies should be responsible for payment.

You may take a friend or relative with you to the hospital for support. In many areas, the hospital will call a rape crisis worker to come and provide you with assistance and support during your hospital experience. Support personnel will also help you arrange transportation home or to another location if you do not feel safe at home.

You may also wish to consider the possibility of psychological counseling to help you recover emotionally from the trauma of the assault. It is easier to recover if you get help right away. You should seek counseling either from a private therapist, your local mental health center, or your local Rape Crisis Center. Many Rape Crisis Centers have discussion groups where you can meet other women who have suffered similar experiences. Most Rape Crisis Centers also offer individual counseling and telephone crisis lines.

You should be aware that you are entitled to speak confidentially about your feelings and your experience to a rape crisis worker. The confidentiality of that communication is protected by law.[28]

Some larger prosecuting agencies like your county attorney's office have social workers who will assist and counsel victims of crime. Call your local county attorney's office to find out if they have a Victim/Witness Counseling Unit.

MUST I GO TO COURT?

If you report the assault to the police and a suspect is caught, you may have to appear in court. (This is not necessary if he pleads guilty to the charge.) You do not need to hire your own lawyer. The case is filed in the name of the state of Utah and the county attorney will handle the case for the state. Technically, you are only a witness in the state's prosecution of the rapist for commission of a public offense.

DO I NEED AN ATTORNEY?

You may want to talk to a private attorney about the possibility of bringing a civil suit against the rapist to obtain a money judgment against him for the damages and suffering he caused you. If you were assaulted on the premises of a "third party" (someone's property other than your own or the rapist's), you may want to ask an attorney if the property owner violated his or her duty to maintain safe premises. For example, there may have been insufficiently secure doors in a hotel or insufficient lighting in a store's parking plaza. You would be the plaintiff in any civil action filed and you would have more control over a civil lawsuit than you have as a witness in the criminal prosecution. There is nothing to prevent you from proceeding with both a criminal prosecution and a civil lawsuit at the same time.

WHAT IF I'M SUBPOENAED?

The victim in a sexual assault case which goes to trial may be subpoenaed to testify at two different proceedings. A subpoena is a legal order for you to appear at a certain time and place. First, you will probably be called to testify at a preliminary hearing before a circuit court judge. The purpose of this preliminary hearing is for the judge to decide if there is "probable cause" to bind the defendant over for trial. All felony cases are tried in the district court. If a guilty plea cannot be arranged in the case, you will need to testify at the trial.

WHAT WILL HAPPEN DURING THE TRIAL?

At trial the lawyer for your attacker may try to show that you consented to sexual intercourse with the defendant. In trying to prove consent, he or she cannot legally introduce evidence of your previous sexual relationships with men other than the defendant.[29] To counter the claim that you consented, the state must be able to show that your attacker used force to overcome your resistance or that you were incapable of resisting the assault.[30] You are not required to have resisted to the full extent of your physical strength if you believed at the time that it would have been useless or if it would have resulted in serious bodily injury. You are only required to demonstrate such "earnest resistance" as could reasonably be expected under the circumstances.[31] The fact that you may have engaged in some friendly social activity—dancing, a drink, conversation, even kissing—with the defendant before the assault does not mean that you lose the right to reject sexual advances.[32]

You do not have to have a witness to the attack. Most often there are no other witnesses to this type of assault. Your testimony alone is sufficient to convict the defendant.

WHAT IS THE PUNISHMENT FOR RAPE?

Rape, object rape, and forcible sodomy, are first-degree felonies, punishable by five years to life in the Utah State Prison and a fine of up to $10,000.

Rape of a child, object rape of a child, sodomy on a child, and aggravated sexual assault are first degree felonies, punishable by five years to life in the Utah State Prison and a fine of up to $10,000, and also requiring that the convicted offender serve a minimum mandatory prison sentence before eligibility for parole.

Forcible sexual abuse and sexual abuse of a child are second degree felonies punishable by one to fifteen years in the Utah State Prison and a fine of up to $10,000.

Unlawful sexual intercourse is a third-degree felony (where the defendant is more than three years older than the victim) punishable by a prison term of zero to five years and a fine of up to $5,000. Unlawful sexual intercourse and sodomy are class B misdemeanors, punishable by up to six months in the county jail and/or a fine of up to $299.[33]

11 Children: Adoption, Support, Protection, Rights of Minors, and Education for the Handicapped

Adoption

HOW CAN I FIND OUT IF I COULD ADOPT A BABY?

In Utah, any minor child (i.e., a person under the age of eighteen years) may be adopted by any adult person, so long as the adopting person is at least ten years older than the adopted child. If a married person wants to adopt a child, the spouse must consent to the adoption. If the child is not orphaned, consent to the adoption must be judicially obtained from both biological parents unless they have legally relinquished custody and guardianship of the child (which happens, for instance, when an unwed mother relinquishes a baby for adoption) or their parental rights have been judicially terminated (as in some child abuse cases). A related situation is when the parents have had no contact with the child or failed to support him or her and the court determines that the child is abandoned.

If the parent or parents of a minor child are themselves minors, they are legally treated as adults in regard to their child. For instance, they may validly relinquish their parental rights or consent to an adoption. If they change their minds later, being minors will not be grounds for revoking the relinquishment.

YOU SAY "PARENTS." WHAT ABOUT GETTING CONSENT FROM THE PUTATIVE FATHER OF A CHILD?

If this baby's biological parents were not married, the father (or man who claims to be the father) may claim rights of paternity by filing a notice with the Department of Health. Forms are available from the registrar of vital statistics or in the offices of any county clerk. The man thus claims (or acknowledges) that he is the child's father and expresses his willingness and intent to support the child to the best of his ability.[1] Once the father has filed this notice, he becomes legally and financially responsible for the child. (He can also be declared the child's father through a paternity suit.)

In either case, however, he would have to claim his rights of paternity before the baby is born but no later than the date the child is relinquished or placed for adoption by the biological mother or the date an adoption petition is filed. If he does not register his claim, he no longer has a legal right to try and establish his paternity. He will also not be able to prevent the child's adoption or relinquishment because, legally, he will be considered to have abandoned the child, waiving any right to notice of proceedings. In cases of "abandonment," the father's consent is not required prior to any adoption or relinquishment.

CAN I ADOPT A BABY IF I'M NOT MARRIED?

Yes. The law states that any adult person (singular) may adopt a child.[2] Thus, a prospective adoption agency cannot deny you a baby simply because you are single. However, since the agency is charged by law to safeguard the child's interests, it may determine—other circumstances being equal—that it's better for a given child to be in a two-parent home. It is best to discuss internal policies frankly with the agency. In any case, the agency will conduct a thorough investigation that includes marital status (married people who have an obviously poor marriage would not be good candidates for a baby), religious background, family constellations, financial position, employment status, personal qualities, and parenting ability.

WHAT ARE THE AGENCIES INVOLVED IN ADOPTION?

No one person or organization may accept or receive a child for adoption who is under the age of eighteen without being licensed by the State Department of Social Services. This department annually reviews every organization, public or private, that is organized as a child placement or adoption agency, for fitness and compliance with the department's standards and regulations. Among these requirements are, as a minimum, that the agency or individual will provide a "secure" home for the child, that it will keep and maintain records of the child's vital statistics, and that it will maintain records of the biological and adoptive parents.[3]

The Salt Lake City phone book lists a half-dozen private adoption agencies in its yellow pages, including church-affiliated agencies. All of these must meet the same state requirements. From there, their services may differ. You should contact each agency to determine its waiting list and get a feeling for how well a particular agency may meet your adoptive needs.

Additionally, the law allows for private arrangements between parties, typically with the assistance of attorneys to be sure that the adoption statutes are met about filing legal documents, appearances in court, etc.[4]

When a private petition for adoption is filed in district court—not through a licensed agency or by a step-parent—the court may order the Division of Family Services to prepare a report within sixty days on the circumstances surrounding the petition: the circumstances of the biological parents, the adoptive parent or parents' financial situation and moral fitness to care for and train the child, the child's physical and mental condition, if it can be determined, and any other factors that may require investigation for the child's welfare.[5] If the report is unfavorable, the court will dismiss the petition and deny the adoption. If the adoption has been processed through a licensed agency, the agency itself will already have conducted the background investigation and determined if the adoption may proceed.

If you are adopting a child born in another state, either through a private party or through an agency licensed in another state, you must meet specific statutory requirements including providing notice of the intent to adopt to the Division of Family Services. No state, agency, or person may send or receive a child until the state receiving the child sends written notice to the "sending" state that it believes the proposed placement to be in the child's best interest.[6]

SAY THAT I'M PREGNANT AND CAN'T KEEP THE BABY BUT DON'T WANT AN ABORTION, HOW COULD I PLACE IT FOR ADOPTION?

You can make the arrangements yourself or have an agency arrange to have the child adopted. Typical sources of adoptive parents are through physicians, hospitals, lawyers, licensed adoption agencies, church organizations, or the State Department of Social Services. Licensed agencies and State Social Services may make arrangements for prenatal care, doctor's appointments, medications, hospitalization, and delivery costs, as well as counseling service.

You and the child's father—if he has acknowledged paternity or is your husband—retain full legal right to the child after birth until a permanent relinquishment has been signed by the natural parent(s). At the same time this permanent relinquishment is given, a temporary custody order will also be filed and signed by the judge or agency, ordering that the adoptive parents assume the "custody, care, and control" of the child pending the final adoption order and decree. This order gives them the legal rights of parents.

The six-months' waiting period is required for the court to be satisfied that this adoption is in the child's best interest and that your consent has been freely given. Then it enters the final adoption order declaring that the child shall henceforth be regarded and treated in all respects as the child of the adoptive parents.[7]

WHAT KINDS OF FINANCIAL ARRANGEMENTS CAN I MAKE IF I DECIDE TO PUT MY BABY UP FOR ADOPTION?

One thing you can't do is "sell" your baby. That's against the law. If someone offers to place your baby in a good home and provide quite a bit of money for you on the side, both of you will be breaking the law. By law, licensed agencies are allowed to charge a "reasonable" fee to cover the costs of their services. If one agency or individual has prices that are excessively high, beware. (This is good advice for adoptive parents, too.)

This does not mean that you have to bear the costs of having the baby alone. It is reasonable for the adoptive parents to provide pre- and post-natal care for you, hospitalization and doctor fees, medication charges, and other necessary expenses incurred as a result of the pregnancy. In some cases, this includes counseling, maternity clothes, and transportation to and from the doctor. It is *not* legal to pay you for having the baby. If you make an agreement to have the baby in exchange for receiving money, you should know that there is no way you can enforce that agreement.

The reason behind this law is that your consent to the adoption must be freely and voluntarily given before the court can enter the order of adoption. If you were to testify that you were desperate for money or were somehow bribed or coerced into agreeing to place the baby, the adoption could be declared invalid. The court would also declare the adoption invalid if you could show that you were "unduly influenced or subjected to duress, fraud, or misrepresentation."

I HAD A BABY AND DECIDED TO KEEP IT, BUT IT'S JUST NOT WORKING OUT. CAN I PLACE A BABY WHO HAS ALREADY BEEN BORN FOR ADOPTION?

Yes, you can relinquish any child for adoption. The law requires that the parent or parents must show the judge that she or they fully and completely understand the significance of their relinquishment.[8]

If you wanted to give up your child, you would file a petition of relinquishment in juvenile court, specifying that you believe it to be in the best interest of both you and the child. It would be very advisable to seek advice from a lawyer or agency to file the proper documents. The judge may require you to do so or may appoint an attorney to assist you. The judge will ask you very specific questions to see if you understand what you're doing and why—chiefly, that in the eyes of the law, you will have no legal claim on or relationship with that child. If the judge is satisfied, he or she will enter an order terminating your rights as a parent. If you relinquish your child, the State Department of Social Services or other agency will become the child's temporary guardian and custodian until, through its own agency, it places the child for adoption.

After the termination order is signed, your parental rights are permanently terminated. Unless you lodge an appeal within thirty days indicating that you had suffered undue influence, duress, fraud, or misrepresentation in agreeing to relinquish, the order will not be overturned and you will be forever deprived of your child. Even if you appeal, the higher court will only review the record of the proceedings to determine whether it shows that you knew and understood the significance of your action. It will not hear additional testimony.[9]

You may also release in writing your parental rights, duties, obligations, care, and control of your child to a licensed agency, thus surrendering the child for placement by that agency. The agency then becomes, in effect, the child's guardian until it is adopted.

WHAT ARE THE STEPS IN ADOPTION?

If you wish to adopt a child you would start looking for a baby by making contacts with various agencies or individuals who do adoptions. A good place to start is by contacting the Department of Social Services at 533-5693.

Initially, it must be determined that the child is legally free to be adopted, then the child will be foot-printed at the sheriff's office to conform to the Missing Children's Act. An attorney will then draw up the necessary legal documents. If you are pregnant and think you would like to place the baby for adoption, you can consent to the adoption or enter into an agreement to release the child, once born, to an adoption placement agency.

As far as the law is concerned, adoption begins when a petition to adopt is filed in the district court, or after July 1985, in the juvenile court in the district in which the adoptive parents reside. If you are adopting the child, you must appear in court to establish the allegations in your petition. The child must also appear in court to consent to the adoption if he or she is over twelve or to enable the judge to form an opinion about the child's best interests.

Because privacy in the case of children adopted as babies is considered important, these court appearances will be at separate times so that the adoptive and biological parents will not see each other.[10]

The judge does two things: he or she ascertains that the adoptive parents agree to treat the child as their own lawful child—to feed, clothe, educate, and support him or her and perform all lawful duties toward him or her. He or she also ascertains that the biological parents freely give their consent for the adoption to take place. When he or she determines that the child's best interests are promoted by the adoption, he or she issues an order approving the adoption. Once the order is issued, in the eyes of the law, the adoptive child cannot be legally distinguished from a biological child.

Usually the child's name is legally changed to that of the adoptive parents unless, in the case of an older child, he or she prefers her birth surname. In the case of infants, a new birth certificate is issued changing only the child's name and its parents' name. The child is given the same surname as its adoptive parents. No other information on the original birth certificate is modified.

Beginning 1 July 1985, adoption-related matters can be handled in either juvenile court or the district court in which the adoptive parents reside. If a licensed agency has not also filed consent to the adoption, the court must—once a petition for adoption is filed—send a copy of the petition to the Division of Family Services within five days to allow them to conduct their background investigation.[11]

It then has sixty days to prepare its background report verifying the allegations of the petition and showing why the biological parents wish to be relieved of the care, support, and guardianship of the child; whether the biological parents have abandoned the child or are morally unfit to have its custody; whether the prospective parents are financially and morally fit to have the child, and any other circumstances which should be considered in the child's best interests.

If a licensed agency has been involved, the "agreement to release to the agency" and the agency's own investigative report are sufficient to enable the court to enter its order, since the agency acts as an arm of the state in conducting its investigation. No report is required from the Division of Family Services.

In the case of a nonagency adoption, the court may accept an affidavit of investigation from the adoptive parents' attorney or may waive investigation altogether.

An adoption petition cannot be granted (the step which makes it irrevocable) until the child has resided with the adopted parents a minimum of six months.

An agreement to adopt is legally enforceable if it is in writing, if the child's biological parents agree with the adoptive parents to relinquish their rights to the child in exchange for the adoptive parents' agreement to adopt, and if there is no intrinsic or extrinsic fraud, undue influence, or duress surrounding the consent to the adoption.

WHAT IF THE BIOLOGICAL PARENTS CHANGE THEIR MINDS?

While there is no law against a biological mother, for instance, changing her mind and revoking consent, the court will only look at the circumstances of the consent to see if it should be set aside. Since the original consent is given in court in the judge's presence or with persons licensed by the State as a child placing agency, it is presumed to be valid and binding. The judge's finding of "knowing and voluntary consent" will not be overturned unless it appeared that he or she acted arbitrarily and capriciously in granting the adoption.[12]

Grounds to revoke consent or to attack an adoption decree must be based on consent wrongfully obtained through fraud, misrepresentation, duress, or undue influence. Requiring the biological mother or parents to give consent is to protect their rights: they must be informed and fully understand the effect of giving consent for the adoption of their child.

CAN I GET COPIES OF THE ADOPTION PROCEEDINGS?

The petition, written investigative reports, and all other documents are sealed and cannot be inspected or copied without the express permission of the court for "good cause." Traditionally, "good cause" has been limited to mean the possibility of hereditary disease or some dire emergency. Curiosity is not sufficient. You must go back to court to get an order to unseal any adoption proceeding.

Child Support

WHAT IS CHILD SUPPORT?

Under the law, parents are responsible to support their children and provide for their care. If you have a child by a first marriage, your second husband is legally obligated to support that child as long as he is married to you. However, the primary responsibility for child support rests with the biological parents (or with adoptive parents) and cannot be contracted away. Failing to support a child is a crime, punishable by jail and/or a fine. It can also be a civil offense, in case of divorce, since a court will have ordered support. Failure to pay can mean that you are in contempt of court and can be fined, jailed, or both.

If the parents have divorced, the court determines the amount of child support according to the circumstances and need at the time of awarding the decree of divorce. (See Chapter 2, "Utah Divorce Law.")

Let's say that your husband has been ordered to pay support and does not do so. You can take him back to court where he will be ordered to pay. If you can't afford to hire a lawyer to help collect back child support, you can apply to the State Office of Recovery Services for help. People there have all the necessary forms and regulations to proceed. Call 483-6100 in Salt Lake City to begin the process of opening a case.

Even if you're receiving some form of public assistance, the Office of Recovery Services will help you collect your child support by getting court orders through the assistance of the county attorney's office for garnishment of wages or other orders which will require your spouse to pay back child support. If a spouse refuses or fails to pay the ordered support, he or she can be prosecuted criminally, which could result in being jailed.

WHAT IF MY HUSBAND HAS LEFT THE STATE?

If you know where to locate him, you can still collect child support. URESA (the Uniform Reciprocal Enforcement of Support Act), passed in 1980, has eliminated conflicts between state laws and provides means to enforce support obligations and collect judgments in other states.

Under URESA, unless you have a private attorney who will do it for you, the county attorney's office will forward the papers they give you to fill out to the appropriate state, along with an affidavit stating the amount of child support owing, broken down month by month, along with a certified copy of the divorce decree which shows the court-ordered amount. The law also empowers the Department of Social Services to garnish wages and empowers the county attorney to divert tax returns for payment of support owing. Be aware that the process of filing on the husband and obtaining a judgment will likely take six months or more because of the backlog of cases.

WHAT IF I WANT TO CHANGE THE AMOUNT OF CHILD SUPPORT THAT MY HUSBAND IS PAYING?

The amount of child support can always be modified—either higher or lower—by either party to the divorce by going back to court. The court will look at the needs of the child and at your husband's ability to pay. Both of you must submit affidavits substantiating the requested increase, including both parties' income and expenses, and the reason for the increase.

You begin the procedure by filing a motion for order to show cause in district court. An order to show cause is served personally on your husband, specifying a date and time for a hearing. At the hearing, the judge will consider the request to modify the amount of child support in the original decree and the evidence supplied in your affidavits. He will adjust the amount if he believes the request is equitable.

If the original child support amount was set by another state, Utah will require that a petition for modification of the original divorce decree be filed. This will require that you obtain certified copies of your divorce papers from the state where you received your divorce.

WHEN DOES CHILD SUPPORT STOP?

Support stops when the child reaches eighteen unless both parties agree to extend support beyond that age for educational purposes or other reasons. You cannot agree to stop support before the age of eighteen.

Crimes Against Children

WHAT ARE CRIMES AGAINST CHILDREN?

As we've just mentioned, failing to support your children can be considered a crime. But usually it is abuse—physical, sexual, or emotional.

Sexual crimes, such as rape are discussed in Chapter 12, "Women and Criminal Justice," along with the special provisions for children (anyone under the age of fourteen). Other crimes against children are encouraging, allowing, or compelling behavior that might contribute to a child's delinquency; willful abuse, neglect, or abandonment; kidnapping or enticing a child away from home or sheltering a runaway; or providing a child with alcohol or a controlled substance. The child need not be convicted of a delinquency before action can be taken against the adult in the case, and all of these actions can be prosecuted as crimes. The degree of crime and therefore the penalty will vary depending on the circumstances.[13]

To term these actions "crimes" means that they have a special legal status: the state has an interest in seeing that they do not occur and will act to protect the child. In a civil offense, a "citizen" has to complain that his or her rights are being offended by the abuse. Since abuse can cause both emotional and physical injury, it is possible to sue the abuser for compensation but this action must be taken by the person who was abused. In a criminal trial, the end result is to punish the offender and the state takes the initiative in prosecuting.

WHAT HAPPENS IF SOMEONE ABUSES A CHILD?

One of the sad things is that nearly always the abuse has to be so severe that someone notices it and reports it—a schoolteacher, a crossing guard, a neighbor who hears a child screaming and crying at night, or an emergency room attendant who becomes suspicious about certain types of injuries. Fortunately, in Utah, it is a crime to know or suspect that a child is being abused or neglected and fail to report it to the police or to the Division of Family Services. The laws against abuse and neglect, in an effort to provide protection for children, specify molestation, incest, sexual exploitation, or sexual abuse as well as physical abuse or neglect.[14] Failure to report suspected abuse or neglect is a class B misdemeanor crime, meaning that you could be subject to six months in jail and/or a fine of $299.[15]

Generally speaking, neglect means that a child is not receiving "proper parental care" because the parent is not able to provide the child with the basic necessities of life such as necessary food, clothing, education, or medical care (including surgery or psychiatric service), and the care necessary for his or her emotional and moral well-being. Abuse means inflicting physical harm or injury on the child.

If you know or suspect abuse or neglect, you are required by law to notify the nearest policeman or law enforcement agency or the Department of Social Services. Any of them will investigate promptly—Social Services is required to investigate within seventy-two hours—and keep your involvement confidential if you wish. If you notify Social Services and if it finds abuse, it is required to notify the police.[16]

If Social Services finds evidence of abuse or neglect, it will have the county attorney's office file a petition alleging abuse or neglect and asking the juvenile court to issue appropriate orders to correct the situation—for the parents to receive treatment, take parenting classes, receive therapy, etc. If the child is actually in danger, Social Services will ask the court to appoint a guardian for the child and has legal authority to remove the child from the abusive or neglectful environment until the circumstances are corrected.[17]

The parents receive a notice that the petition has been filed, complete with a hearing date. They are entitled to be represented by an attorney, court-appointed, if necessary, in these proceedings. They are also entitled to request a trial, where the state is required to prove its allegations that abuse or neglect has occurred.[18]

If the parents admit their abuse or neglect or if the court finds sufficient evidence for abuse or neglect, it will enter its order requiring the parents to take treatment and to be accountable to the court, through Social Services, for improving the conditions of the children's environment.

This particular type of proceeding is not considered criminal, and the juvenile court judge does not have authority to jail or fine anyone. However, if the child or children have been removed from the home or if the court orders that they continue to stay in foster care while the parents receive treatment, the parents can be ordered to pay some or all of the costs of the care for the child outside the home.

In other cases, if the parents or someone brings an injured child to a doctor or hospital, they may, by law, keep a child for up to seventy-two hours in protective custody if there is reason to suspect abuse or neglect and if, as well, there is reason to believe that the child's safety will be in danger without protective custody. Again, if a child is retained in protective custody, Social Services is immediately notified and a court order of temporary custody or protective supervision must be obtained to retain the child longer than seventy-two hours.

Even if the doctor or hospital does not exercise protective custody, Social Services must be notified of suspected abuse or neglect and can request follow-up written reports within forty-eight hours of the oral report.

Cases involving children can frequently involve two courts: the juvenile court which has jurisdiction over actions involving abuse or neglect of children and the child's interests and the criminal courts which prosecute the offender.

All reports of suspected abuse or neglect are confidential and anyone who releases data or information obtained in the investigation can be charged with a class C criminal misdemeanor, which carries the penalty of ninty days in jail or a $299 fine or both.[19]

WHAT CRIMINAL PROCEDURES TAKE PLACE?

Although legal definitions and the penalties are spelled out in Chapter 12, many of the sexual crimes against children carry mandatory prison sentences. In these provisions, Utah is like most states in the Union.

If a person has been charged with a felony involving a child sexually (for example, unlawful sexual intercourse, rape, object rape, sodomy, or sexual abuse), the penalties may include a minimum mandatory term of three, six, or nine years, or life imprisonment, if the crime was aggravated.[20]

However, Utah law is unique in that if special circumstances exist and the sexual offense involving the child is not considered legally to be "aggravated,"[21] the court may suspend the prison sentence and impose probation and treatment instead.

These conditions are:

1. The person must be in a "position of trust" with the child, that is, a parent, step-parent, or legal guardian.
2. In the offense, he or she acted alone, did not use weapons or force, and did not injure the child.
3. There are no prior offenses involving sexual misconduct.
4. The offense did not involve pornography, prostitution, or sex with anyone else.

5. It is in the victim's best interests that the defendant not be imprisoned.
6. He or she has been accepted for mental health treatment at a sexual abuse clinic and rehabilitation through treatment is probable.
7. He or she will not live at home for one year.
8. He or she spends at least thirty days in jail and is on probation for ten years maximum.

I WAS SEXUALLY ABUSED BY MY STEPFATHER AS A CHILD BUT NO ONE EVER KNEW. AS AN ADULT, DO I HAVE ANY LEGAL RECOURSE OR RIGHT TO TREATMENT?

The law provides that you can only file criminal charges within one year of when you first learned about the abuse, not necessarily one year from the time it happened.

The cut-off point for filing a civil suit for emotional distress is two years from the time it occurred. Get advice from an attorney if you aren't sure about your circumstances.

Rights of Minors

HOW OLD DO I HAVE TO BE TO GET MARRIED?

In Utah, you have to be over eighteen or else have the permission of your parent or guardian to apply for a marriage license. (If you've been married before and are under eighteen, you are considered an adult in applying for a second marriage license.) If you are under sixteen and get married without parental consent, the marriage is not only illegal but is considered void from the beginning.

WHAT ABOUT GETTING AN ABORTION?

If you are under eighteen, you cannot receive contraceptive services or get an abortion from a publicly funded institution without the written consent of your parent or guardian unless you are married, a member of the armed forces, or otherwise emancipated. Emancipation means you have been declared independent either with or without consent of parents or by the court.

For further discussion of these issues, see Chapter 9 "Mental and Physical Health."

Education for Handicapped Children

WHAT IS THE "EDUCATION FOR ALL HANDICAPPED CHILDREN ACT"?

The Education for All Handicapped Children Act, commonly referred to as Public Law 94-142, guarantees every school-age handicapped child a free and "appropriate" public education.

Handicapped, according to the law, refers to the condition of a child who has a physical or mental disability that interferes with his or her ability to participate in or benefit from education programs. Examples include children who are deaf, hard of hearing, visually handicapped, mentally retarded, orthopedically impaired, learning disabled, speech impaired, autistic, or seriously emotionally disturbed.

Special education programs involve both specially designed instruction which will meet the unique educational needs of the child and related services. These services include speech therapy, occupational therapy, counseling services, transportation, and any other support services needed to help the child participate in school.

Every school district must locate all handicapped children who live within the district, and every handicapped child must be given a complete evaluation to determine the extent of the child's handicap. Then, special education must be provided according to an individualized education plan (IEP). The IEP is the written plan that describes the child's educational program and is developed at a meeting among the parents, teacher, and an administrator from the child's school. Parents have an equal voice in developing their child's IEP.

If parents disagree with the school district's identification, evaluation, or placement of their child or believe that appropriate and necessary educational or related services are being denied, they may request a due-process hearing. An impartial hearing officer will be appointed to hear the evidence and determine if the child is receiving appropriate educational or related services.

If you have any questions concerning Public Law 94-142, you can call the Legal Center for the Handicapped at 363-1437 or 1-800-662-9080.

12 Women and the Military

WHAT DOES THE MILITARY HAVE TO DO WITH ME?

Women may interact with the military in a number of ways. You may become involved as an active duty member of one of the armed services, join the reserves or national guard, or be the wife or dependent of an active duty member. In each instance, you will have certain rights and benefits as a result of the particular way you are affiliated. This chapter highlights some pertinent areas.

Remember that military recruiters will give you additional information, but their job is to get you to join. Therefore, they may paint an overly rosy picture. The VA office nearest your home can also provide information on benefits for former members of the military.

CAN I BE DRAFTED?

The draft was abolished in this country in 1973. This means that under *existing* legislation, women cannot be drafted into military service. Neither can men.

In 1981, Congress approved legislation requiring all male United States citizens and resident aliens in a certain age group to register under the Military Selective Service Act unless they were exempt for medical or other reasons. Although no laws prohibit registering women for military service, Congress has never chosen to do so. The United States Supreme Court has ruled that exempting women from registration for the draft is not unconstitutional. That is, it *is* legal to draft men and not draft women.

These registration laws are presumably intended to give the military a list of eligible candidates who may be called for active service if Congress reinstitutes the draft. Congress would have to pass new legislation to require women to register with the selective service. Additional legislation would also be needed to reestablish the draft for men or women.

WHAT POSITIONS MAY I HOLD IN THE MILITARY?

Even though the military had traditionally been an exclusively male organization, recent years have seen dramatic changes. Today, women constitute 10 percent of the active force and 1.7 percent of the reserve components. As officers and enlisted personnel filling traditional and nontraditional roles, they serve in a wide variety of jobs. Equal opportunity for women, as well as minorities, is an integral part of policy for the military today. The army's policy illustrates that of the other services:

a. The policy of the United States Army is to provide equal opportunity and treatment for uniformed members and their families irrespective of race, color, religion, sex, or national origin and to provide an environment free of sexual harassment. This policy—
   1. Applies both on and off post.
   2. Extends to soldiers and their families.
   3. Applies to soldiers' working, living, and recreation environments (including both on- and off-post housing).

b. Soldiers will not be accessed, classified, trained, assigned, promoted, or be otherwise managed on the basis of race, color, religion, sex, or national origin *except*—
   1. As the direct combat probability coding policy applies to women. . . . (U.S. Army Regulations 600 - 20 dated 1978, revised 15 Oct. 1980.)[1]

This exception currently prohibits women from serving in combat-related military occupational specialties (MOS). A few MOS's closed to women include infantryman, combat engineer, and atomic demolition munition specialist.

The prohibition extends to assigning women to combat units as well. In the Naval Service, women may be assigned to noncombatant ships which provide various support elements to United States Naval warships. Currently, women may not be assigned to warships.

Women may attend the Naval, Army, and Air Force academies. They may also become military officers through ROTC programs or Officer Candidate School (OCS). With the equal opportunity policies of today's military, career paths have never been better for women in the armed services, whether it be officer or enlisted.

WHAT ABOUT SEXUAL HARASSMENT?

Because of the traditional male military environment, women in the armed services have suffered instances of sexual harassment. In this regard, the military is mirror of the rest of society.

The military has taken an active role in fighting sexual harassment. Army policy is typical of the other services:

Sexual harassment is an unwelcome form of sex discrimination. It is not limited to the work environment and can occur at almost any place. Sexual harassment violates acceptable standards of integrity and impartiality required of all Army personnel and interferes with mission accomplishment and unit cohesion. Many of the acts and neglects that constitute sexual harassment are prohibited and punishable under civil and military law as criminal acts of a sexual nature, and should be treated as such. Any military member or civilian employee is engaging in sexual harassment who—

a. Through behavior of a sexual nature attempts to control, influence, or affect the career, pay, or job of a military member of civilian employee.
b. Makes deliberate or repeated verbal comments or gestures of a sexual nature that are offensive to the person to whom addressed.
c. Makes abusive physical contact of a sexual nature. (U.S. Army Regulation 600-21 dated 1 Feb. 1984.)

Women in the military are encouraged to report acts of sexual harassment. Military authorities are instructed to take immediate action to investigate and eliminate such demoralizing behavior.

WHAT IS FRATERNIZATION?

Closely allied to the problem of sexual harassment is fraternization. Although fraternization has not always been clearly defined, it basically involves improper relationships between senior and junior ranking individuals.

Central to any discussion of the propriety of a particular relationship of members of different rank is the authority or influence one servicemember has over the other.

Certain structures within the military demand closer regulation of relationships because of the greater risk that they will involve partiality or an abuse of authority or the appearance of either. These include, for example, basic combat training, military schools, combat units in training, etc.

Therefore, when the senior has direct command or supervisory authority over the lower ranking member or has the capability to influence personnel or disciplinary actions, assignments, or other benefits or privileges, there is the strongest justification for exercising restraint on social, commercial or duty relationships.

The present army fraternization policy developed to reflect the changing relationships—especially dating—between members of different rank or grade is a predictable and reasonable consequence of more women entering the service. It could reasonably be predicted that young women would date and marry senior soldiers because women date, on an average, men two to four years older. Another reasonable expectation was that more dating would take place in the same unit because people tend to date people from their work place. Dating is not, in general, considered improper. However, the possibility and the opportunity for abuse is very real. Unlike the old fraternization custom, current army custom has been broadened beyond officer-enlisted relationships to include all relationships between members of different ranks. It acknowledges that any social, commercial, or duty relationship may result in an impropriety.

Relationships between servicemembers of different rank which involve (or give the appearance of) partiality, preferential treatment, or the improper use of rank or position for personal gain, are prejudicial to good order, discipline, and high unit morale. Such relationships will be avoided. Commanders and supervisors will counsel those involved or take other action, as appropriate, if relationships between servicemembers of different rank—

1. Cause actual or perceived partiality or unfairness,
2. Involve the improper use of rank or position for personal gain, or,
3. Can otherwise reasonably be expected to undermine discipline, authority, or morale. (U.S. Army Regulation 600-20, para. 5-7f, dated 15 Oct. 1980.)

This policy is based on common sense and good judgment. An association between an officer and an enlisted member might not amount to the criminal offense of fraternization, but it might be considered inappropriate. Just because a certain relationship is not unlawful does not mean that it is appropriate. This is true in many aspects of military life. Any relationship between military members that reflects partiality or unfairness, improper use of rank or position, or which undermines discipline, authority, or morale is prohibited by policy.

For example, a male officer arranging for special leave for an enlisted girlfriend so they can spend a weekend together might well be improper.

IS IT MORE DIFFICULT TO GET MARRIED IF I AM IN THE MILITARY?

It is important to understand that military policy and national security take precedence over the needs of individuals. If you join the service and subsequently marry a serviceman, there is no guarantee that you will continue to be assigned to the same duty stations. Some of the services try to transfer couples together, but they are not required to do so. The key word is need. Where do they need you?

If you become pregnant on active duty, you may seek a voluntary honorable discharge and it will be granted, regardless of your marital status. However, you cannot be involuntarily discharged from the service merely because you are pregnant, married or not.

You must remember that when you join the service, you sign a legally binding contract that obligates you for a specific number of years. After you join, it is very difficult to get out until you have successfully completed your tour of duty. Early discharges often result in an unfavorable military discharge and/or record which can follow you for life. Hence, you should make a decision to join the military and/or marry in the military only after careful deliberation.

WHAT EFFECT MIGHT A DIVORCE HAVE ON MILITARY RETIRED PAY?

For many years, wives of servicemen could not claim any property interest in the retirement benefits their husbands earned. This was perceived as a gross inequity.

In 1982 Congress enacted the Uniformed Services Former Spouses Protection Act,[2] effective 1 February 1983, which allows state courts to consider retired pay of military personnel when adjudicating property rights between parties in a divorce proceeding. Here are its key provisions:

1. The act does not require you to have been married for a minimum period before a state court is entitled to divide military retired pay.
2. The act provides that up to 50 percent of retired pay may be awarded as either marital or community property in a single divorce case.

3. Once you receive a court-ordered interest in retired pay, it becomes a lifetime interest. Even if you remarry, you still get it.
4. In some cases for marriages of over ten years, the act lets the military send you the check directly.
5. You are entitled to full medical, commissary, and exchange rights if your marriage covered twenty years of military service. However, courts cannot order that you be designated beneficiary under the Survivor Benefit Plan (SBP).
6. The act may be applied retroactively. Divorce judgments within a division of retired pay rendered before 26 June 1981 may now be enforced. Divorce judgments decided after that date without a division of retired pay may now be modified to include it.

IS DIVORCE LEGALLY DIFFERENT IN THE MILITARY?

No. Support orders, alimony, and child support can be and are enforced against military pay. Federal law now allows a court to garnish military wages to pay child support or alimony or similar obligations under a separation agreement. This is true for reserve or national guard pay as well as active duty pay. Local laws prevail and different states regulate how much or what percentage of the pay can be garnished.

Federal law also allows garnishments for past amounts as well as current obligations. Consequently, if a servicemember fails to pay support in violation of a court order, you can collect these past-due amounts.

WHAT IS THE SOLDIERS' AND SAILORS' CIVIL RELIEF ACT?

Congress enacted this act at the beginning of World War II to help civilians mobilized into the military, either voluntarily or involuntarily.[3] The basic idea is not to penalize you because you are in military service; but at the same time, you should not have an unfair advantage because of it.

Some of its benefits apply not only to the person who is entering on active military service, but also to his or her dependents and those to whom the serviceperson owes money. The protection begins when you receive orders to report for extended active duty and it ends a short period of time after separation from military service.

This relief is not automatic. For example, when some form of legal action—like a lawsuit—affects your rights, *ordinarily*, you must "trigger" the act by calling the court's attention to the fact that the Soldiers' and Sailors' Civil Relief Act may apply to you. Your attorney can do this for you. If the court decides that military service did *materially affect* your ability to comply, it will grant appropriate relief under the act.

HOW DOES THE ACT PROTECT ME?

It may provide temporary relief in a variety of situations. For example, if you are not present to defend yourself in a lawsuit, it prevents the court from awarding a default judgment. A landlord cannot evict your spouse and dependents for nonpayment of rent if it's under $150 a month. (The act says "wife," but the courts have generally been sex-neutral in applying it.) It can temporarily halt mortgage foreclosures on property you and your spouse or dependents own. It delays payments required under installment sales contracts made before you entered active duty as well as payment on interest on debts or contracts acquired before entry on active duty. The act also temporarily stops fines and penalities imposed under the terms of most contracts.

This is only a brief summary of parts of the act. In general, if you or someone acting on your behalf applies, the court will intervene and temporarily suspend proceedings or provide other appropriate relief such as restructuring payment schedules, extending time for payment, etc.

In addition, there may be other situations where the act will help you. Ask an attorney for more information. Since many civilian lawyers are not familiar with military law, try to contact a military lawyer (JAGC Officer) or a civilian lawyer who specializes in military law. The State Bar referral service should have a list of lawyers with such experience.

CAN I GET MY CIVILIAN JOB BACK AFTER I'M OUT OF THE MILITARY?

Usually. If you join the military, or are drafted, you have the right to be restored to your former position or one of similar status, seniority, and pay. You are also entitled to receive automatic pay increases which have been granted other employees during your absence. This law covers private, federal, state, county, and city employees.[4]

To be eligible for your former position, you must meet the following requirements:

1. The employment was not temporary.
2. You left only because of your military service.
3. You did not serve more than four years active duty.
4. You are qualified to perform the duties of the position. If you were disabled in the service and cannot perform your former duties, you are entitled to receive the nearest comparable job with duties you can perform.
5. You must apply for restoration within ninety days after your release from active duty. If you are hospitalized, you have up to ninety days after your release from post-discharge hospitalization as long as you are not hospitalized more than one year.

IF I AM IN THE RESERVES OR NATIONAL GUARD, ARE THE PROVISIONS DIFFERENT?

No. You are entitled to the same job protection for part-time military service as well.

Chapter 432, Title 38 of the *United States Code* stipulates, with some specialized exceptions:

1. Your employer is required to excuse you from work for military training.
2. You cannot be discharged because you are in the Reserve Components, or because you seek time off for military training.
3. You cannot be denied promotion because of your Guard or Reserve status.
4. Your employer cannot subtract your military training from your vacation time.
5. Your employer cannot limit the number of times you are required to perform military training.
6. As long as you are not gone longer than four years (five years as a federal employee), you are entitled to your old job or its equivalent.

WHAT BENEFITS DO DEPENDENTS RECEIVE?

Your husband and children can use military exchanges or commissaries (stores), theaters, clubs, and other facilities, including the hospital and dental clinics. There are many regulations about medical care. Before you join, you should get detailed information about the medical benefits your family would be entitled to. This information is available at any military post or at CHAMPUS (Civilian Health and Medical Program of the Uniformed Services) in Denver, Colorado 80240. Also see Department of Defense Pamphlet Pa-3B, "Uniformed Services Health Benefits Program."

Generally, your husband and children under twenty-one are entitled to use medical facilities on a military post. If there is no space or facility available or if they are not living near a military installation, they are entitled to use a civilian facility at government expense under the CHAMPUS program. Not all facilities will accept dependents under this program. Also, there are some expenses which you must pay.

CHAMPUS is a cost-sharing program designed to help you pay for authorized medical services obtained from civilian sources. When you and your dependents are not living together, they are not required to first seek medical care from a military facility. However, it is important when your dependents receive medical care from a civilian physician or hospital to, determine at the outset, that the caregiver will accept the CHAMPUS reimbursement as full payment for his charges. (CHAMPUS has a fee schedule for all types of services.) If not, then your dependents must pay the difference between what the physician or hospital charges and the CHAMPUS reimbursement.

Get detailed information about your dependents before you need it.

Another benefit to dependents is that they (and you) can get free legal advice and help from any military installation with a Legal Assistance Office. It is very useful to get an expert opinion on planned legal actions such as signing a contract. The Legal Assistance Officer cannot represent your dependents on some types of legal problems, such as representation on criminal charges, lawsuits between private parties, or lawsuits you may want to file against the military or federal government, but, even there, he can help them in finding a civilian lawyer.

13 Jury Duty

HOW ARE JURORS SELECTED?

Under Utah law, prospective jurors for county and state courts are selected county by county from the official register of voters for each voting district in the county. This master list is periodically updated to include the names of persons registered to vote in the most recent general election. Thus, if you are registered to vote, your name is on the master list and you are eligible to be called as a juror. In addition to registered voters, the master list may be supplemented by names from other sources as directed by the Utah Supreme Court. Other sources might include property tax rolls and drivers' license records. These would be used, however, only in the unlikely event that all names on the master list were exhausted.

Prospective jurors are to be selected at random from a fair cross-section of the population of the area served by the court. No citizen may be excluded or exempted from jury duty because of race, color, religion, sex, national origin, or economic status.

AM I QUALIFIED TO BE A JUROR?

Not everyone on the master list is qualified to serve as a juror. Utah law requires that jurors be citizens of the United States, over eighteen, registered to vote, residents of the county, and be able to read, speak, and understand English. The court determines whether prospective jurors are qualified. It bases its decision on the information provided on the juror qualification forms, interviews with prospective jurors, or other evidence as needed. Furthermore, a person may *not* serve who has been convicted of a felony, is on active duty in the military, or is not capable of rendering satisfactory jury service because of physical or mental disability.

IF I AM SELECTED, WHAT IS THE PROCEDURE?

You will receive in the mail a juror qualification form from the clerk of the court. The purpose of this form is to let the court determine whether you are qualified to serve as a juror based on the seven requirements shown above. You must complete and return this form to the clerk within ten days after it is received, *even if you think you are not qualified to serve as a juror*. It is up to the court to determine whether you are qualified. If you have a mental or physical disability, you may be required to submit a physician's certificate to verify the disability.

Any person who fails to properly complete and return a jury qualification form or who willfully misrepresents a material fact on the form may be fined up to $500 and/or imprisoned for up to 30 days.

MAY I BE EXCUSED FROM JURY DUTY?

Jury duty is one of a citizen's responsibilities—and a very important one. You represent the community in determining guilt or innocence in the case you will hear. However, under certain circumstances, you may be excused from jury duty even if you are otherwise qualified.

To be excused, you must show undue hardship, extreme inconvenience or public necessity. For example, an excuse of severe illness in your immediate family requiring your presence at home will usually be sustained. Or if you own your own business and receive a call to jury duty during your busiest season, you can usually be excused or at least have your time of jury service postponed. Should your job be one of public necessity (important to the day-to-day functioning of the community) like a doctor, pharmacist or fireman, you can request to be excused from jury service. It is up to the court to decide, based on your request, whether to excuse you from jury duty.

WHAT ABOUT JURY DUTY IN FEDERAL COURTS?

Any qualified citizen can be called to serve on a jury for a federal as well as a state or county court. The selection process is basically the same. From the list of voters who voted in the last general election, the county jury commission composes a master list of prospective jurors. At the request of a judge, the clerk of the court randomly selects a panel of jurors from the master list and sends each of them a juror qualification form to fill out.

However, in addition to the qualifications of the state courts, a juror in a federal court must have lived in the judicial district at least a year. Also, anyone with a charge pending against her or him in a state or federal court of record for a crime punishable by imprisonment for more than a year is not qualified.

You are exempt from federal court jury duty if you are in active service in the armed forces, in a police or fire department, or are a public official—elected or appointed, actively performing official duties in executive, legislative, or judicial offices of federal, state, or local governments. For instance, if you are a county recorder, you would be exempt. If you are a secretary in the county recorder's office, however, you would be eligible.

You may also be excused by individual request showing that jury service would create "extreme inconvenience or undue hardship" for you. For example, if you had to spend more than an hour traveling to court you could probably be excused. A mother of young children can usually be excused. For other examples of extreme inconvenience and undue hardship, please refer to the preceding section of this chapter entitled "May I Be Excused From Jury Duty?"

You may be qualified and offer no excuses but still be excluded from serving on the jury of a particular case. You and the other prospective jurors will be placed under oath and questioned by the judge and/or lawyers to determine your qualifications to serve as jurors for the case about to be tried. The purpose of this "voir dire" examination is to obtain an impartial unbiased jury. Following voir dire, the final selection of the jury begins. The lawyers for each side "challenge" jurors they find objectionable to their side.

A challenge is a request that a juror be excused. Challenges are either "for cause" or "peremptory." A challenge for cause is based upon some specific fact known about a juror which disqualifies him or her for the case at hand. Some possible reasons you may be challenged for cause include a prior relationship between you and one of the parties, your prejudice or prior knowledge regarding the case, or the fact that you may stand to benefit in some way by a decision for one side or the other. There is no limit to the number of challenges for cause, but the judge decides whether each one is accepted or rejected.

A peremptory challenge can be made for no reason at all. Lawyers rely on their experience and "hunches" as to the type of juror who would be best for each client's case. A lawyer may excuse you peremptorily simply because he dislikes the way you sit or smile. Unlike challenges for cause, the number of peremptory challenges is strictly limited by law.

WHAT KIND OF CASES COULD I BE ASKED TO SERVE ON?

Juries in Utah hear both criminal and civil cases. Criminal cases are controversies between the state and an accused individual. Civil cases are controversies between individuals concerning matters like contracts, accidents, debts, etc. In criminal cases, juries decide whether the accused is guilty and whether he or she is to be deprived of life or liberty. Upon a guilty verdict, the judge, in most cases, determines how long the sentence will be. In civil cases, juries decide not only who the winner is, but how much he or she wins.

A jury trial may last a few hours, a day, a week, several weeks or, on rare occasions, several months. Jurors are not sequestered (isolated from contact with the public) in Utah. They are allowed to go home at night during the trial but are cautioned not to read newspapers, watch television, or discuss the trial with anyone.

The same jury panel never hears more than one case, although individual jurors may serve on more than one jury during their term of jury service.

WHAT IF I GET SICK WHILE I'M SERVING?

You, of course, would be excused from jury duty should you become ill during the trial. What would happen next depends on the type of case your jury is deciding.

In a felony case that might be long, Utah law provides for an alternate juror. The alternate is selected at the same time and in the same manner as the original jurors. He or she must attend the trial at all times and hear and see everything the original jurors do. If an original juror dies or becomes ill before the case is submitted to the jury for a decision, the alternate juror assumes the juror's place and is bound by the same rules.

Utah law requires unanimous jury verdicts in criminal cases. So, in a criminal trial where no alternate juror has been selected, the illness of a juror could result in a mistrial. This would mean that the lawyers would have to appear again at a later date, select a new jury, and present their case all over again.

In civil cases, three-fourths of the jurors may reach a verdict, so the illness of one juror need not necessarily result in a mistrial.

HOW WILL JURY SERVICE AFFECT MY JOB?

Not at all. Utah law forbids your employer from threatening, coercing, or firing you because you are either called as a juror or serve on a jury. If your employer threatens to fire you or fires you when you are summoned for jury duty, you should contact a lawyer. He or she could be held in criminal contempt which could result in a fine of up to $500 and/or up to six months in prison. If your employer fires you, you may bring a civil suit within thirty days for your wages and to obtain an order reinstating you in your job.

WILL I BE COMPENSATED FOR JURY DUTY?

Yes, you will receive fifteen cents a mile for travel from home to court and back. You will also receive $14 a day for each day you are required to attend court sessions.

HOW OFTEN AM I ELIGIBLE FOR JURY DUTY?

If you are being considered as a prospective juror, you are only required to attend ten court days (usually Mondays through Fridays, excluding holidays). If you are selected for a jury, however, you must complete your service for that particular case.

If you serve on a trial jury or a grand jury (which is a jury called to decide whether there is enough evidence to require an accused person to stand trial), you are not eligible to serve again for two years.

14 Utah's Equal Rights Statutes

DOES THE UTAH CONSTITUTION PROHIBIT DISCRIMINATION BASED ON SEX?

Yes. Utah's Constitution includes an equal rights provision which guarantees that:

The rights of citizens of the State of Utah to vote and hold office shall not be denied or abridged on account of sex. Both male and female citizens of this State shall enjoy equally all civil, political and religious rights and privileges.[1]

Although the provision specifically emphasizes the right to vote and hold office, its reference to sexual equality in civil and religious rights provides general protection from discrimination on the basis of sex.[2]

ARE THERE OTHER ANTI-DISCRIMINATION PROVISIONS IN UTAH LAW?

Yes. The Utah Anti-Discriminatory Act[3] and the Utah Civil Rights Act[4] aim at eliminating discrimination in public places and in the employment arena. (Some specifics are discussed in Chapter 7, "Employment," in this handbook.)

WHAT KIND OF PROTECTION DOES THE ANTI-DISCRIMINATION ACT PROVIDE?

The major thrust of the Utah Anti-Discriminatory Act is to prevent an employer from hiring, firing, promoting, or compensating any person on the basis of race, color, sex, religion, ancestry, national origin, handicap, or age (if the individual is forty years of age or older). Businesses *can* consider such factors as sex, age, handicap, or religion where those factors are bona fide or genuine occupational qualifications necessary to the operation of the business; but the burden of proof is on the business. For example, a business would not be required to hire a handicapped person whose handicap would make it dangerous for her to do the work. Similarly, a private school operated by a particular church would not be required to hire someone of a different religious belief to teach its religion classes.

The Utah Supreme Court has stated that the purpose of this act is to eliminate discrimination in the payment of wages based *solely* on the basis of sex where men and women are doing the same or similar work under similar conditions. There are, however, circumstances which could validly justify a difference in wages.[5] Consideration must be given to the class or grade of the employee, education, seniority, and the degree of responsibility the employee is required to assume.

According to the act, if you feel you have been harmed by a discriminatory employment practice, you may file a written complaint with the Utah State Industrial Commission which will then investigate the complaint. If the complaint cannot be settled by mutual agreement of the parties, a hearing will be held. At the conclusion of the hearing, the complaint will be dismissed or the employer will be ordered to stop the discriminatory practice and to provide you with appropriate affirmative relief.

WHAT KIND OF PROTECTION DOES THE UTAH CIVIL RIGHTS ACT PROVIDE?

The function of the Utah Civil Rights Act is to assure all citizens, regardless of sex, race, color, religion, ancestry, or national origin, equal access to all goods, services, and facilities offered by business establishments, places of public accommodation, and enterprises regulated by the state. This would include every place, establishment, or facility that caters or offers its services, facilities, or goods to the general public for a fee or charge. By definition, the act has no effect upon any facility, church, club, or apartment house which is private and not open to the public.

If a business or place of public accommodation or enterprise regulated by the state is found to be operating in a discriminatory manner, it will be legally ordered to stop the prohibited practices. Any individual, corporation, or organization which denies a person full and equal access may be liable for damages or other appropriate relief.

WHAT IS THE STATUS OF THE NATIONAL "E.R.A."?

In 1972, Congress approved the Equal Rights Amendment, the proposed amendment to the U.S. Constitution which provided that "equality of rights under the law shall not be denied or abridged by the United States or by any State on account of sex." Thirty-five states ratified the amendment, but approval was needed by three more states before 30 June 1982 to make the ERA part of the Constitution. Such ratification failed to occur. At this writing, legislators are drafting a new Equal Rights Amendment to submit to Congress.

Notes

Chapter 2

1. UCA §30-3-l (1953) as amended (also incl. UCA §30-3-2).

2. Id.

3. UCA §30-4-l (1953) as amended (also incl. UCA §30-4-3 and §30-4-5).

4. Id.

5. UCA §30-1-17 (1953) as amended.

6. UCA §30-1-2 (1953) as amended.

7. UCA §30-1-1 (1953) as amended.

8. UCA §30-1-2(4) & (5) (1953) as amended.

9. UCA §30-1-2 (1953) as amended (also UCA §30-1-9).

10. UCA §30-3-7 (1953) as amended 1985.

11. UCA §30-3-10 (1953) as amended.

12. *Kallas v. Kallas*, 614 P.2d 641, 645 (Utah 1980).

Chapter 3

1. *Peterson v. Peterson*, 571 P.2d 1360, 1361 (Ut. 1977).

2. Id.

3. Utah Constitution, Art. XXII, §2.

4. UCA §30-2-1, 30-2-5 (l953).

5. UCA §30-2-1 (1953).

6. UCA §3-2-6.

7. UCA §30-2-8.

8. UCA §30-2-9.

9. *Boise Cascade Corp. v. Meyer*, 568 P.2d 755, 756 (Ut. 1977); See also, *Gee v. Baum*, 58 Utah 445, 199 P. 680 (1921).

10. UCA §75-2-113 (1953).

11. UCA §75-2-201 *et seq.* 207.

12. Id.

13. UCA §75-2-201.

14. UCA §75-2-201,-202.

15. UCA §75-2-202.

16. UCA §75-2-502.

17. UCA §75-2-505(2).

18. UCA §75-2-503.

19. UCA §75-2-201, 207.

20. UCA §75-6-103, 106.

21. UCA §75-6-101(14).

22. UCA §75-6-104(3).

23. UCA §75-2-102.

24. UCA §75-2-103.

25. UCA §75-2-104.

26. UCA §75-2-107.

27. UCA §75-2-108.

28. UCA §75-2-112.

29. UCA §75-2-109(a).

30. UCA §75-2-109(b).

31. For a general discussion of the factors considered by the courts in determining the validity of antenuptual and postnuptual agreements, see, *Scherer v. Scherer* 249 Ga. 635, 292 S.E.2d 662 (1982), an antenuptial case. Utah's position appears to be that courts, while not bound to abide by postnuptual agreements between spouses in determining property settlements, should respect them and give them great weight. See, *Mathie v. Mathie*, 12 Utah 2d 116, 363 P.2d 779 (1961); *Pearson v. Pearson*, 561 P.2d 1080 (Utah 1977); *Naylor v. Naylor*, 563 P.2d 184 (Utah 1977). Utah courts are likely to apply this same theory to antenuptial agreements.

Chapter 4

1. Title 11 of the United States Code (USC). The new code is effective for cases filed after 30 September 1979.

2. 11 USC §101(9) (1978).

3. 11 USC §101(4) (1978).

4. 11 USC §362 (1978), as amended by P.L. 98-353 (1984).

5. 11 USC §101(31), as amended by P.L. 98-353 (1984).

6. 11 USC §101(41), as amended by P.L. 98-353 (1984).

7. 11 USC §522 as amended by P.L. 98-353 (1984).

8. The Bankruptcy Code gives each state the authority to impose its scheme of exemptions upon a debtor in bankruptcy rather than giving the debtor a choice between state and federal plans. In its 1981 session, the Utah legislature exercised this authority. The Utah exemptions statute is found in UCA §§ 78-23-1 to 78-23-15 (Supp. 1981).

9. 11 USC §302 (1978).

10. 11 USC §1301 (1978), as amended by P.L. 98-353 (1984).

11. 11 USC §727 (1978), as amended by P.L. 98-353 (1984).

12. 11 USC §523 (1978), as amended by P.L. 98-353 (1984).

13. 11 USC §523(a)(2) (1978), as amended by P.L. 98-353 (1984).

14. 11 USC §523(a)(1) (1978), as amended by P.L. 98-353 (1984).

15. 11 USC §524(a) (1978), as amended by P.L. 98-353 (1984).

16. 11 USC §524(c) (1978), as amended by P.L. 98-353 (1984).

17. 11 USC §1328 (1978), as amended by P.L. 98-353 (1984).

18. 11 USC §727(a)(8) (1978).

Chapter 5

1. But see, *Sex Bias in the U.S. Code: A Report of the U.S. Commission on Civil Rights*, (1977).

2. R. Crouch, *The Legal Status of the Homemaker in Virginia*, (1977).

3. IRC §143; Treas Reg. §1.143-1 (1971).

4. Rev. Rul. 76-255, 1976-2C.B.40.

5. IRC §2-b Treas. Reg §1.2-2-b.

6. IRC §143, 6013-(d); Treas. Reg. §1.2-2-1971; Treas. Reg. §1.143.1-(b); Treas. Reg. §1.6013-4(a).

7. Rev. Rul. 58-66, 1958-1 C.B.60.

8. IRC §§2(a), 143, 6013(d); Treas. Reg §§1.2-2(a), 1.6013-4(a).

9. IRC §6013(f).

10. IRC §85.

11. IRC §2513(d).

12. IRC §6013(e); Treas. Reg. §1.6013-5 1974.

13. IRC §151(b); Treas. Reg. §1.151-1(b) 1972.

14. IRC §152; Treas. Reg. §1.152-4 1971.

15. Rev. Rul. 78-91, 1978-1 C.B.36, amplifying Rev. Rul. 73-175, 1973-1 C.B.58.

16. Treas. Reg. §1.262-1 (b) 1972.

17. IRC §212(1); *J. U. Elliot*, 40 T.C. 304 1963; *R. K. Wild*, 42 T.C. 706 1964.

18. IRC §215.

19. Rev. Rul. 76-344, 1976-2 C.B.82.

20. Rev. Rul. 73-200, 1973-1 C.B.140, superseding Rev. Rul. 67-339, 1967-2 C.B.126.

21. Rev. Rul. 73-201, 1973-1 C.B.140.

22. Rev. Rul. 73-603, 1973-2 C.B.76.

23. Rev. Rul. 55-261, 1955-1 C.B.307, modified by Rev. Rul. 68-212, 1968-1 C.B.91.

24. IRC §21, Treas. Reg. §1.44A, 1985.

25. IRC §71, Treas. Reg. §1.71-1, 1957.

26. See, e.g. *United States v. Davis*, 307 U.S. 65 1962.

27. Treas. Reg. §1.71(d).

28. Rev. Rul. 74-153, 1974-1 C.B.20.

29. Rev. Rul. 59-5, 1959-1 C.B.12.

30. IRC §85.

31. Rev. Rul. 70-217, 1970-1 C.B.12.

32. IRC §101; Treas. Reg. §1.101-1, 1964.

33. IRC §101; Treas. Reg §1.101-2, 1976.

34. Rev. Rul. 70-281, 1970-1 C.B.16.

35. Rev. Rul. 55-330, 1955-1 C.B.381-34.

36. Rev. Rul. 72-605, 1972-2 C.B.35.

37. IRC §2503(b).

38. IRC §2513.

39. IRC §§2010, 2505.

40. IRC §2522.

41. IRC §§2201-2210.

42. IRC 2011.

43. IRC 2056.

Chapter 6

1. 42 USC §§402-431.

2. 42 USC §414; 20 CFR §§404.101-110.

3. 20 CFR §404.410(a).

4. 42 USC §402-w.

5. 20 CFR §404.330(d).

6. 42 USC §423-d-1-A and §1382c-a-3-A.

7. 20 CFR §404.1520.

8. *Weinburger v. Weisenfeld*, 420 U.S. 636 (1975). Formerly only women were entitled to these "mother's benefits"; under this decision a father can now receive payments on the same basis widowed mothers have in the past.

9. See note 2.

10. 42 USC §415(b); 20 CFR §404.212.

11. 20 CFR §404.130-b-c-d.

12. 20 CFR §422.110.

13. 20 CFR §404.330.

14. 20 CFR §404.335.

15. 42 USC §402-e.

16. 20 CFR §404.332-b-6.

17. 20 CFR 416.110.

18. 42 USC §1381 et seq; 20 CFR §416.101-416.2119.

19. 42 USC §§1395 et seq; 20 CFR.

20. Utah Department of Social Services Assistance Payments Administration Volume II (Financial Assistance) §§218-222.8; §§240-242; §§306-338; §§400-440.

21. Utah Department of Social Services Payments Administration Volume II (Financial Assistance) §§218-222.8; §§240-242; §§306-338; §§400-440.

22. APA Volume II (Financial Assistance) §§502-560.

23. Utah Department of Social Services Assistance Payments Administration Volume IV (Food Stamps) §650.

24. APA Volume IV (Food Stamps) §650.

25. Unemployment compensation, UCA §35-4-1 et seq (1953).

26. UCA §35-4-3 (1953).

27. *Turner v. Dept. of Employment Security*, 423 U.S. 44 (1975).

28. Utah Worker's Compensation Act, UCA §35-1-1 et seq. (1953).

Chapter 7

1. *De Santis v. Pacific Telephone and Telegraph Co.* 608 F.2d 327 (9th Cir. 1979).

Chapter 9

1. UCA §26-17-6 et seq.

2. 42 USC §2681-2688.

3. UCA §26-17-15 (1979), §64-7-6 (1967).

4. UCA §64-8-13 (1983).

5. UCA §64-7-29 (1975).

6. UCA §64-7-31 (1979).

7. UCA §64-7-36(1) (1981).

8. UCA §64-7-36(10) (1981).

9. UCA §64-7-48(1) (1979).

10. UCA §75-5-201(18) (1979).

11. UCA §75-5-303 (1975).

12. UCA §75-5-312 (1977).

13. UCA §75-5-303 (1975).

14. UCA §75-5-401 (1985).

15. UCA §75-5-212 (1975).

16. UCA §64-7-46 (1979).

17. UCA §64-7-48 (1979).

18. UCA §64-7-47 (1979).

19. UCA §26-25-1 (1981), §78-24-8 (1984).

20. UCA §76-7-323 (1981).
21. UCA §64-10-1 through 64-10-16 (1983).
22. UCA §64-10-1(1) (1983).
23. UCA §64-10-1(2) (1983).
24. UCA §64-10-7 (1983).
25. UCA §64-10-11 (1983).
26. UCA §64-10-8(1) (1983).
27. UCA §64-10-8(3) (1983).
28. UCA §64-10-8(4) (1983).
29. UCA §64-10-14 (1983).
30. *Roe v. Wade*, 410 U.S. 113 (1973).
31. UCA §76-7-302(1) (1978).
32. UCA §76-7-301(3) (1986 Supp.) and 302(2) (1978).
33. UCA §76-7-302(3) (1978).
34. *Harris v. McCrae*, 448 U.S. 297 (1980).
35. UCA §76-7-304(2); *H.L. v. Matheson* 450 U.S. 398 (1981).
36. *Planned Parenthood Assoc. of Utah v. Matheson*, 582 F.Supp. 1001 (1983).

Chapter 10

1. UCA §7-5-402-1.
2. UCA §76-5-407-2.
3. UCA §76-5-402.1-1.
4. UCA §76-5-406.
5. UCA §76-5-402.1-2.
6. UCA §76-5-401-0.
7. UCA §76-5-401-2.
8. UCA §76-5-402.2.
9. UCA §76-5-403.1.
10. UCA §76-5-404.
11. UCA §76-5-403-3.
12. UCA §76-5-403-2,-3.
13. UCA §76-5-403.1-1.
14. UCA §76-5-403.1.2.
15. UCA §76-5-403.
16. UCA §30-1-2.7.
17. UCA §76-5-406.
18. UCA §76-5-406.

19. UCA §§76-5-404.1.

20. UCA §76-5-404-2, UCA §76-5-404.1-2.

21. UCA §76-5-404-2, UCA §76-5-404.1-2.

22. UCA §76-5-407.

23. UCA §76-5-406-1, -2, -3, -7.

24. Susan Brownmiller, *Against Our Will: Men, Women and Rape* (1975) New York: Simon and Schuster, Inc.

25. Salt Lake Rape Crisis Center Statistics, 2035 South 1300 East, Salt Lake City, Utah 84105 (801-467-7273).

26. Department of Justice, *FBI Uniform Crime Reports* (1976), p. 16.

27. Id., p. 16.

28. UCA §78-3C-1, §78-24-8.

29. *State v. Johns*, 615 P.2d 1260 (Ut. 1980).

30. *State v. Meyers*, 606 P.2d 250 (Ut. 1980).

31. *State v. Herzog*, 610 P.2d 1281 (Ut. 1980).

32. *State v. Stettina*, 635 P.2d 75 (Ut. 1980).

33. UCA §76-5-401 *et. seq.*; §76-3-203, §76-3-204, §76-3-301.

Chapter 11

1. UCA §78-30-4(3).

2. UCA §78-30-1.

3. UCA §55-8a-1.

4. UCA §78-30-8.

5. UCA §78-30-14.

6. UCA §55-8b-1.

7. UCA §78-30-9.

8. UCA §18-3a-48.

9. UCA §78-30-4.

10. UCA §76-30-6.

11. UCA §70-30-14.

12. UCA §78-30-8.

13. UCA §78-3a-19.

14. UCA §78-3b-3.

15. UCA §78-3b-10.

16. UCA §78-3b-6.

17. UCA §78-3b-8.

18. UCA §78-3a-16.

19. UCA §78-3b-13.

20. UCA §75-5-404.1.

21. UCA §76-5-406.5.

Chapter 12

1. Army regulations available at any army installation.

2. *Title X*, USC §1072, 1076, 1086.

3. 50 App USC §§501 et seq.

4. Veterans Reemployment Act, 38 USC §20-21.

Chapter 14

1. Utah Const. Art. IV, Sec. 1.

2. See *Kopp v. Salt Lake City*, 29 Utah 2d 170, 172, 506 P.2d 809, 810 (1973), in which the court took the position that Article IV, Sec. 1 of the Utah Constitution is a "clear and comprehensive statement . . . that there shall be no discrimination based on sex."

3. UCA §34-35-1, 1953 & Supp. 1981.

4. UCA §13-7-1, 1953 & Supp. 1981.

5. *Kopp v. Salt Lake City*, 506 P.2d at 809-10.

Resources for Further Help

AMERICAN CIVIL LIBERTIES UNION (ACLU)
632 Judge Building, #8 East Broadway
Salt Lake City, Utah 84111 Phone: 521-9289

HOURS: 9:00 a.m.-5:00 p.m.

PURPOSE: To defend the Bill of Rights through litigation, legislation, and public education. Litigation is limited to precedent setting and class-action cases.

SERVICES: Assesses complaints for their potential of advancing goals and objectives of the organization and provides direct representation when these conditions are met. Makes referrals, when possible, for other types of problems.

FEES: None

ORGANIZATION STATUS: Private, nonprofit

BETTER BUSINESS BUREAU OF GREATER SALT LAKE
1588 South Main Street
Salt Lake City, Utah 84115 Phone: 487-4656

HOURS: 8:30 a.m.-5:00 p.m.
(9:30 a.m.-4:00 p.m. by telephone)

PURPOSE: To provide information concerning the business community locally and out-of-state. Assists with complaints concerning local businesses, mail orders, magazine subscriptions, etc.

SERVICES:
1. Advisory services.
2. Public information.
3. Investigation of reports on businesses.

FEES: None

ORGANIZATION STATUS: Private, nonprofit

CONSUMER CREDIT COUNSELING SERVICE OF UTAH, INC.
220 East 3900 South, Suite #1
Salt Lake City, Utah 84107 Phone: 266-0064

HOURS: 9:00 a.m.-5:30 p.m.

PURPOSE: To help overindebted families with budgeting and money management.

SERVICES:
1. Budgeting and personal money management help.
2. Educating families on the wise use of credit.
3. Setting up a "composition of debt" plan for liquidating indebtedness.
4. Referring families to other agencies when necessary.

FEES: Variable, up to $10 per month

ORGANIZATION STATUS: Private, nonprofit

FAMILY SUPPORT CENTERS

PURPOSES: Prevention and treatment of child abuse.

SERVICES: 1. 24-hour crises resident services for children, up to age eight, who are abused or in danger of being abused.
2. Parenting skills classes.
3. Parenting counseling.

FEES: Sliding fee scale for counseling services.

ORGANIZATION STATUS: Private, nonprofit. Department of social services contact service provider.

Child & Family Support Center
149 West 300 North
Logan, Utah 84321
723-8591

Family Support Center
622 - 23rd Street
Ogden, Utah 84401
626-3300

The Family Support Center
2020 Lake Street
Salt Lake City, Utah 84105
487-8000

The Family Support Center
75 West Center Street
Midvale, Utah 84047
487-8000

Family Support Center
1141 West Antelope Drive
Layton, Utah 84041
776-6112

Utah Valley Family Support
206 East 300 South
Provo, Utah 84601
373-6154

INDUSTRIAL COMMISSION OF UTAH

160 East 300 South
Salt Lake City, Utah 84110 Phone: 530-6800

HOURS: 8:00 a.m.-5:00 p.m.

PURPOSE: To provide better working conditions, especially in matters of safety and labor relations, and compensation for workers injured in industry. To handle all forms of employment discrimination.

SERVICES: 1. Industrial Safety: OSHA consultation (533-7927) and OSHA Division, 448 South 400 East (533-6401).
2. Labor Division for problems arising relative to workers under 18 and women workers (533-5971).
3. Wage Claim Division (533-6411).
4. Worker's Compensation Division for questions arising from on-the-job injuries (533-5641).
5. Anti-discrimination unit (630-6922).

FEES: None

ORGANIZATION STATUS: Public

LEGAL AID SOCIETY OF SALT LAKE

231 East 400 South - lower level
Salt Lake City, Utah 84111 Phone: 328-8849

HOURS: 8:30 a.m.-5:00 p.m.

PURPOSE: To provide legal assistance to the poor.

SERVICES: 1. Emergency legal services for abused spouses, regardless of income.
2. Domestic relations.
3. Creditor-debtor relations: bankruptcies handled on a very limited basis according to need, but other counseling and lawyer services offered in many debtor-creditor matters which can be handled without bankruptcies.
4. Consumer matters.
5. Welfare, landlord/tenant, social security appeals.

SATELLITE: Copperview Community Center 8446 Harrison Street (340 West) Salt Lake City, Utah 84047 HOURS: 1:30 p.m.-4:00 p.m. (Thursday afternoons)

FEES: None

ORGANIZATION STATUS: Private, nonprofit

LEGAL CENTER FOR THE HANDICAPPED
455 East 400 South, Suite 300
Salt Lake City, Utah 84111 Phone: 1(800)662-9080; 363-1347

HOURS: 8:30 a.m.-5:00 p.m.

PURPOSES: To provide legal council for disabled persons having problems related to physical or mental handicaps.

SERVICES: 1. Legal services to developmentally disabled individuals dealing with problems that arise because of their handicapping conditions.
2. Referrals to appropriate agencies.

FEES: Sliding scale

ORGANIZATION STATUS: Private, nonprofit

LEGAL DEFENDER ASSOCIATION, SALT LAKE
333 South 200 East
Salt Lake City, Utah 84111 Phone: 532-5444

HOURS: 8:00 a.m.-5:00 p.m.

PURPOSE: To represent indigent individuals in criminal cases. Must be appointed by the courts.

SERVICES: 1. Legal representation in courts of Salt Lake County.
2. Advice on criminal cases, bail reduction.

FEES: None

ORGANIZATION STATUS: Public

LEGAL SERVICES, INC., UTAH
637 East 400 South
Salt Lake City, Utah 84111 Phone: 328-8891

HOURS: 8:30 a.m.-5:00 p.m.

PURPOSES: To provide legal services to low income clients on civil legal matters.

SERVICES: 1. Senior Law Services (Over age 55).
2. Landlord/tenant services.

3. Claims with public agencies.
4. Civil legal problems (will not handle criminal cases).

FEES: None. Donations accepted.

ORGANIZATION STATUS: Private, nonprofit

PHOENIX INSTITUTE
383 South 600 East
Salt Lake City, Utah 84102 Phone: 532-5080

HOURS: 8:00 a.m.-5:00 p.m.

PURPOSE: To offer alternative career choices through prevocational training, career exploration, and counseling programs.

SERVICES:
1. Prevocational training and placement services for low income women (CETA & WIN).
2. On-the-job training in skilled trades and non-traditional jobs.
3. Transition Center: career counseling, resume writing.

FEES: Dependent upon economic status.

ORGANIZATION STATUS: Private, nonprofit

RAPE CRISIS CENTER, INC., SALT LAKE
776 West 200 North
Salt Lake City, Utah 84116 Phone: 532-7273

HOURS: 8:00 a.m.-5:00 p.m. (24-hour hotline)

PURPOSE: To help victims and families cope with the trauma of rape. To provide educational and preventative services to the community.

SERVICES:
1. 24-hour crisis line with trained volunteers. Will meet with individuals when indicated.
2. Escort and advocacy service. Volunteers accompany victim to the hospital and provide support through the medical, police and legal proceedings.
3. Information and referral services.
4. Education: speakers bureau and education/prevention programs for grade school students.
5. Support services: self-defense classes. Rap groups.

FEES: None

ORGANIZATION STATUS: Private, nonprofit

SOCIAL SERVICES, UTAH STATE DEPARTMENT
150 West North Temple (Administrative Office)
Salt Lake City, Utah 84145-0500 Phone: 533-7305

HOURS: 8:00 a.m.-5:00 p.m.

PURPOSE: The Department of Social Services is the largest department in State Government. It includes six divisions (Division of Aging and Adult Services; Division of Alcoholism and Drugs; Division of Family Services; Division of Services to the Handicapped; Division of Mental Health, Division of Youth Corrections) and four offices (Office of Recovery Services; Office of Assistance

Payments; Office of Community Operations and Statewide Offices of Community Operations) It also includes two State Institutions (Utah State Hospital, Utah State Training School).

The Department of Social Services provides a variety of services through its thirteen offices of community operations throughout the state. The staff in these offices determine eligibility for state and federal programs, and provide services to clients by contract and direct services. Services available to clients in all districts include adoptions, aging and adult services, aid to families with dependent children, day care, energy assistance, emergency work programs, family and individual counseling, food stamps, foster care, homemaker, medicaid, protective services to children and adults, self-sufficiency, services to the handicapped, and social service health plan case management. In some districts the office also provides direct services for mental health, alcohol and drugs and services under the county medically indigent program. If you experience problems with services at the community level you may call a toll-free number for the Department of Social Services (1-800-662-3722) and discuss the difficulty.

District Offices

District 1 (Cache, Rich, Box Elder)
1050 South 500 West
P. O. Box 1000, Brigham City, Utah 84302
Phone: 723-8591

Sub Offices:
129 North 1st West
Logan, Utah 84321
Phone: 752-2511 (DFS Services Only)

95 W. 1st South
Logan, Utah 84321
Phone: 753-2511 (APA Services Only)

Rich County Courthouse
P. O. Box 417
Randolph, Utah 84064
Phone: 793-2015

125 South 1st West
Tremonton, Utah 84337
Phone: 257-0123;

24-Hour on Call Number:
Logan, 752-0750; Brigham City, 723-3421

District 2A (Morgan, Weber)
385 24th Street, P. O. Box 349
Ogden, Utah 84402
Phone: 621-8270

24-Hour on Call Number:
Ogden, 309-1371

District 2B (Salt Lake Central District)
2835 South Main
P. O. Box 15729
Salt Lake City, Utah 84115
Phone: 487-8000

Sub Offices:
554 South 300 East
Salt Lake City, Utah 84111

24-Hour On Call Number:
Phone: 487-9811

District 2C (Davis)
1350 East 1450 South
P. O. Box 825
Clearfield, Utah 84015
Phone: 776-6112

Sub Offices:
470 East Medical Drive
Bountiful, Utah 84010
Phone: 295-4665 and 295-9474
Child Abuse - Phone: 544-1298 (After Hours)

24-Hour On Call Number:
Davis County - Phone: 544-1298

District 2K (Salt Lake Valley West District)
4115 West 5295 South
Kearns, Utah 84118
Phone: 969-7201 (DFS Services only)

Sub Offices:
4095 West 5295 South
Kearns, Utah 84118
Phone: 969-6304 (APA Services only)

55 North Redwood Road, Suite A
Salt Lake City, Utah 84104
Phone: 533-4310

24-Hour On Call Number:
SL West, 487-9811; SL North, 487-9811

District 2S (Salt Lake South Valley District)
7292 South State
Midvale, Utah 84047
Phone: 255-8475

24-Hour On Call Number:
SL South, 487-9811

District 2T (Tooele)
47 South Main, Room 300
Tooele, Utah 84074
Phone: 882-5550, 355-1539 (SL Direct)

Sub Offices:
255 South 1st East
Tooele, Utah 84074
Phone: 882-3323 (MH Svcs.)

59 East Vine
Tooele, Utah 84074
Phone: 882-2870

P. O. Box 1180, Wendover, Utah 84083
Phone: 665-2231(2)

24-Hour On Call Number:
Tooele, 882-2022

District 3 (Utah, Wasatch, Summit)
260 West 3rd North
P. O. Box 1464
Provo, Utah 84603
Phone: 373-6154 (DFS Services only)

Sub Offices:
305 North 500 West
P. O. Box 777
Provo, Utah 84603-0811
Phone: 377-2800 (APA Services Only)

89 North 100 East
Heber City, Utah 84032
Phone: 654-1541

1753 Sidewinder Drive
P. O. Box 680247
Park City, Utah 84068
Phone: 649-6018

24-Hour On Call Number:
Provo, 373-6327

District 4 (Juab, Piute, Millard, Sanpete, Sevier, Wayne)
201 East 5th North
Richfield, Utah 84701
Phone: 896-8476

Sub Offices:
50 South Main, Suite 5
Manti, Utah 84642
Phone: 835-2861/835-6731

Main & Courthouse
P. O. Box 12
Nephi, Utah 84648
Phone: 623-1927

20 East 1st North
P. O. Box 589
Fillmore, Utah 84631
Phone: 743-6611 (DFS)
Phone: 743-5304 (APA)

252 West Main
P. O. Box 280
Delta, Utah 84624
Phone: 864-3869

24-Hour On Call Number:
Sevier, 896-6433; Juab, 623-1344; Millard, 864-2755; Sanpete, 662-1526

District 5 (Beaver, Iron, Washington, Garfield, Kane)
551 South 3rd East
P. O. Box 880
St. George, Utah 84770
Phone: 673-9691

Sub Offices:
1552 West 2nd North
P. O. Box 309
Cedar City, Utah 84720
Phone: 586-3841

190 North 100 East
P. O. Box 72
Beaver, Utah 84713
Phone: 438-2443

110 West Center
P. O. Box 172
Kanab, Utah 84741
Phone: 644-5885

565 North Main
P. O. Box 395
Panguitch, Utah 84759
Phone: 676-8866

24-Hour On Call Number:
St. George, 662-1778

District 6 (Duchesne, Daggett, Uintah)
1052 West Market Drive
Vernal, Utah 84078
Phone: 789-5850

Sub Offices:
855 East 2nd North (112-3)
Roosevelt, Utah 84066
Phone: 722-4594

(Mental Health) 722-4625
Professional Plaza
Duchesne, Utah 84021
Phone: 738-2494

24-Hour On Call Number:
Uintah, Daggett, 789-5528; Duchesne, 722-4474

District 7A (Carbon, Emery, Grand)
90 North 1st East
Price, Utah 84501
Phone: 637-6850

Sub Offices:
45 East 100 South
P. O. Box 697
Castle Dale, Utah 84513
Phone: 381-2387

150 West 200 South
Moab, Utah 84532
Phone: 259-6128 (DFS)

24-Hour On Call Number:
Carbon-Emery, 637-1621;
Grand, 259-8115 (This is the Sheriff's office and they have a pager for the on-call worker.)

District 7B (San Juan)
522 North 100 East
Blanding, Utah 84511
Phone: 678-3211

Sub Offices:
San Juan County Courthouse
Monticello, Utah 84535
Phone: 587-2016 (Info. & Referral)

24-Hour On Call Number:
San Juan, 678-2036

The Office of Recovery Services

Salt Lake Office
Administration
3269 South Main Street
Salt Lake City, UT 84115
(801) 377-6206

Salt Lake Office
(Operations)
3195 South Main Street
Salt Lake City, UT 84115
(801) 483-6100

Brigham City Office
1050 South 500 West
P. O. Box 1000
Brigham City, UT 84320
(801) 734-9871

Ogden Office
533 26th Street
Ogden, UT 84401
(801) 627-0540

Provo Office
1665 West 820 North
Provo, UT 84601
(801) 483-6100

Richfield Office
201 East 500 North #8
Richfield, UT 84701
(801) 896-5461

Farmington Office
2125 South 2nd West
P. O. Box 699
Farmington, UT 84025
(801) 451-5087

St. George Office
551 South 300 East #106
St. George, UT 84770
(801) 628-1732

Vernal Office
1052 West Market Drive, #13
Vernal, UT 84078
(801) 789-5855

FEES: Dependent upon economic status
ORGANIZATIONAL STATUS: Public

UTAH ISSUES INFORMATION PROGRAM
231 East 100 South
Salt Lake City, Utah 84111 Phone: 521-2035

HOURS: 8:00 a.m.-5:00 p.m.

PURPOSE: An advocacy agency to represent a coalition of low-income residence and agencies working to increase their representation in local, state, and federal decision-making processes.

SERVICES:
1. Advocacy on behalf of residents to help them achieve necessary services at the government levels.
2. Active engagement in state policy evelopment in areas of social services, housing, employment, education, and taxation with government staff and elected officials.

FEES: None

ORGANIZATION STATUS: Public

UTAH STATE BAR ASSOCIATION
425 East 100 South
Salt Lake City, Utah 84102 Phone: 531-9077

HOURS: 9:00 a.m.-5:00 p.m.

PURPOSE: Professional organization required of all lawyers practicing in the state. Supervised by the Bar Commission of Utah.

SERVICES: Provides a referral service for persons seeking legal advice.

FEES: Lawyer's fees

ORGANIZATION STATUS: Private, nonprofit

VICTIM WITNESS SERVICES

Salt Lake County Attorney's Office
450 South 300 East
Salt Lake City, Utah 84111 Phone: 363-7900

HOURS: 8:30 a.m.-5:00 p.m.

PURPOSE: To aid victims of crime to help resolve their crises. Target population: children and elderly. Emphasis on violent assault, sexual assault, and spouse abuse.

SERVICES:
1. Crisis and supportive counseling.
2. Referral and long-term counseling.
3. Support through criminal justice system.

FEES: None

ORGANIZATION STATUS: Public

YOUNG WOMEN'S CHRISTIAN ASSOCIATION OF SALT LAKE CITY (YWCA)

322 East 300 South
Salt Lake City, Utah 84111 Phone: 355-2804

HOURS: 8:00 a.m.-5:00 p.m. — programs vary

PURPOSE: To promote a safe and healthy environment for women and children who are living within domestic violence. To provide education, information and support that can assist women in making informed choices about their lives.

SERVICES: Residence for battered women and their children. Women in Jeopardy Program, 24-hour crisis service.

Crisis Homes

Logan:	752-2511 Family Services 752-0750 Family Services 752-4600 Sheriff
Price:	637-6850 Family Services 637-1621 Sheriff
Provo:	377-5500 Center for Women & Children in Crisis
Vernal:	789-5850 Family Services 789-5528 Crisis Line 789-4222 Police
Ogden:	621-8270 Family Services 392-7273 Women's Crisis Center 394-9456 YMCAM
Cedar City:	586-3841 Family Services
St. George:	673-9691 Family Services

FEES: None

ORGANIZATION STRUCTURE: Private, nonprofit